TEACHER'S PET PUBLICATIONS

PUZZLE PACK
for
The Catcher in the Rye
based on the book by
J. D. Salinger

Written by
William T. Collins

© 2005 Teacher's Pet Publications
All Rights Reserved

The materials in this packet are copyrighted
by Teacher's Pet Publications, Inc.

These pages may be duplicated by the purchaser
for use in the purchaser's own classroom.

Copying any of these materials and distributing them
for any other purpose is a violation of the copyright laws.

© 2005 Teacher's Pet Publications, Inc.
www.tpet.com

INTRODUCTION
If you already own the LitPlan for this title, this Puzzle Pack will refresh your Unit Resource Materials and Vocabulary Resource Materials sections plus give you additional materials you can substitute into the tests. If you do not already have a complete LitPlan, these pages will give you some supplemental materials to use with your own plan. There are two main groups of materials: one set for unit words (such as characters' names, symbols, places, etc.) and one set for vocabulary words associated with the book.

WORD LIST
There is a word list for both the unit words and the vocabulary words. These lists show you which words are being used in the materials and the clues or definitions being used for those words. You may want to give students a word list with clues/definitions to help them, or you may want students to only have a word list (without clues/definitions) if you want them to work a little harder. Both are available for duplication. The word lists can also be your "calling key" for the bingo games.

FILL IN THE BLANK AND MATCHING
There are 4 each of the fill in the blank and matching worksheets for both the unit and vocabulary words. These pages can be used either as extra worksheets for students or as objective parts of a unit test. They can be done individually if students need extra help or as a whole class activity to review the material covered.

MAGIC SQUARES
The magic squares not only reinforce the material covered but also work on reasoning and math skills. Many teachers have told us that their students really enjoy doing these!

WORD SEARCH PUZZLES
The word search words go in all directions, as indicated on your answer keys. Two of the word search puzzles have the clues listed rather than the words. This makes the puzzle a little more difficult, but it reinforces the material better. Two word search puzzles have words only for students who find the clue puzzles too difficult.

CROSSWORD PUZZLES
Both unit and vocabulary word sections have 4 crossword puzzles.

BINGO CARDS
There are 32 individual bingo cards for the unit words and 32 individual bingo cards for the vocabulary words. You can use your word list as a "call list," calling the words at random and marking them off of your list as you go, or you could use the flash cards by cutting them apart and drawing the words at random from a hat (or box or whatever). To make a better review, you might ask for the definition and spelling of each word as you call it out–or you could call out the definitions and have students tell you the words they need to look for on the puzzle.

JUGGLE LETTERS
The vocabulary juggle letter game is intended to help students learn the spellings of the words. One sheet has the definitions listed on it as an extra help for students who need it or to reinforce the definitions if you choose to do so.

FLASH CARDS
We've included a set of vocabulary flash cards you can duplicate, cut, and fold for your students. Some teachers make a few sets for general use by the class; others make a set for each student. Some teachers duplicate them for each student and have the students cut & fold their own. You can cut out just the words and put them in a hat, have each student pick out one word and write the definition and a sentence for that word. Students then swap words and papers, with the next student adding a sentence of his own under the last one. You can have students swap as many times as you like. Each time the student will read the sentences written prior to his own and then add a sentence. You can cut out the words and definitions separately and play "I Have; Who Has?" Each student in the room draws a word and definition. The first student says, "I have (the name of the word). Who has the definition?" The student with the definition reads it then says, "I have (the name of the vocabulary word she has). Who has the definition?" The round continues until all words and definitions have been given.

Catcher In The Rye Word List

No.	Word	Clue/Definition
1.	ACKLEY	Roomed next to Holden at Pencey
2.	ACTORS	According to Holden, these people were the biggest phonies of all
3.	ALLIE	Holden's dead brother
4.	ANTOLINI	English teacher
5.	BAGS	Phoebe packed hers so she could go with Holden
6.	BEANS	Little Shirley ___; record Holden bought Phoebe
7.	CAROUSEL	Holden watched Phoebe ride one
8.	CASTLE	James ____ committed suicide
9.	CATCHER	The ___ In The Rye
10.	CAULFIELD	Narrator; Holden
11.	CHRISTMAS	Season to be jolly
12.	ERNIE	Holden lied to his mother on the train
13.	FAILED	Holden was kicked out of Pencey because he ___
14.	FENCING	Holden returned to school with the ___ team
15.	GALLAGHER	Checker-playing neighbor friend of Holden: Jane ___
16.	GLOVE	Topic of the composition Holden wrote for Stradlater
17.	IMMATURE	An ___ man wants to die nobly for a cause.
18.	LAVENDER	Bernice and friends danced with Holden at the ___ Room
19.	LUCE	Student at Whooton; had a drink with Holden
20.	MAURICE	Elevator operator who set Holden up with Sunny
21.	MORON	Holden calls people this when they do things that don't suit him
22.	MUSEUM	Holden liked it because everything there stayed put
23.	NOSE	Stradlater gave Holden a bloody one
24.	NUNS	Holden chatted with them at the sandwich bar
25.	PENCEY	The school
26.	PHOEBE	Holden's sister
27.	POEMS	Allie's glove had these written on it
28.	SALINGER	Author
29.	SALLY	Holden's theater date
30.	SIMMONS	Lillian; DB's old girlfriend
31.	SPENCER	History teacher
32.	STRADLATER	Holden's roommate who was good-looking but conceited
33.	SUNNY	The prostitute
34.	TRAIN	Holden's transportation to NY

Catcher In The Rye Fill In The Blank 1

1. Topic of the composition Holden wrote for Stradlater
2. Little Shirley ___; record Holden bought Phoebe
3. The ___ In The Rye
4. According to Holden, these people were the biggest phonies of all
5. Holden calls people this when they do things that don't suit him
6. Holden's roommate who was good-looking but conceited
7. Roomed next to Holden at Pencey
8. An ___ man wants to die nobly for a cause.
9. Stradlater gave Holden a bloody one
10. Season to be jolly
11. Holden watched Phoebe ride one
12. Holden was kicked out of Pencey because he ___
13. Student at Whooton; had a drink with Holden
14. The school
15. Author
16. Bernice and friends danced with Holden at the ___ Room
17. Lillian; DB's old girlfriend
18. English teacher
19. Holden chatted with them at the sandwich bar
20. Holden liked it because everything there stayed put

Catcher In The Rye Fill In The Blank 1 Answer Key

Answer	Clue
GLOVE	1. Topic of the composition Holden wrote for Stradlater
BEANS	2. Little Shirley ___; record Holden bought Phoebe
CATCHER	3. The ___ In The Rye
ACTORS	4. According to Holden, these people were the biggest phonies of all
MORON	5. Holden calls people this when they do things that don't suit him
STRADLATER	6. Holden's roommate who was good-looking but conceited
ACKLEY	7. Roomed next to Holden at Pencey
IMMATURE	8. An ___ man wants to die nobly for a cause.
NOSE	9. Stradlater gave Holden a bloody one
CHRISTMAS	10. Season to be jolly
CAROUSEL	11. Holden watched Phoebe ride one
FAILED	12. Holden was kicked out of Pencey because he ___
LUCE	13. Student at Whooton; had a drink with Holden
PENCEY	14. The school
SALINGER	15. Author
LAVENDER	16. Bernice and friends danced with Holden at the ___ Room
SIMMONS	17. Lillian; DB's old girlfriend
ANTOLINI	18. English teacher
NUNS	19. Holden chatted with them at the sandwich bar
MUSEUM	20. Holden liked it because everything there stayed put

Catcher In The Rye Fill In The Blank 2

_____

1. Elevator operator who set Holden up with Sunny
2. Holden's transportation to NY
3. The school
4. Holden was kicked out of Pencey because he ___
5. An ___ man wants to die nobly for a cause.
6. Holden's theater date
7. Holden's sister
8. Holden liked it because everything there stayed put
9. Lillian; DB's old girlfriend
10. Little Shirley ___; record Holden bought Phoebe
11. Holden's roommate who was good-looking but conceited
12. Holden's dead brother
13. Student at Whooton; had a drink with Holden
14. Author
15. Narrator; Holden
16. James ___ committed suicide
17. Holden chatted with them at the sandwich bar
18. Holden watched Phoebe ride one
19. Stradlater gave Holden a bloody one
20. Checker-playing neighbor friend of Holden: Jane ___

Catcher In The Rye Fill In The Blank 2 Answer Key

MAURICE	1. Elevator operator who set Holden up with Sunny
TRAIN	2. Holden's transportation to NY
PENCEY	3. The school
FAILED	4. Holden was kicked out of Pencey because he ___
IMMATURE	5. An ___ man wants to die nobly for a cause.
SALLY	6. Holden's theater date
PHOEBE	7. Holden's sister
MUSEUM	8. Holden liked it because everything there stayed put
SIMMONS	9. Lillian; DB's old girlfriend
BEANS	10. Little Shirley ___; record Holden bought Phoebe
STRADLATER	11. Holden's roommate who was good-looking but conceited
ALLIE	12. Holden's dead brother
LUCE	13. Student at Whooton; had a drink with Holden
SALINGER	14. Author
CAULFIELD	15. Narrator; Holden
CASTLE	16. James ___ committed suicide
NUNS	17. Holden chatted with them at the sandwich bar
CAROUSEL	18. Holden watched Phoebe ride one
NOSE	19. Stradlater gave Holden a bloody one
GALLAGHER	20. Checker-playing neighbor friend of Holden: Jane ___

Catcher In The Rye Fill In The Blank 3

1. Holden calls people this when they do things that don't suit him
2. Allie's glove had these written on it
3. Holden returned to school with the ___ team
4. Holden watched Phoebe ride one
5. An ___ man wants to die nobly for a cause.
6. Checker-playing neighbor friend of Holden: Jane ___
7. Holden lied to his mother on the train
8. Holden liked it because everything there stayed put
9. Holden's roommate who was good-looking but conceited
10. According to Holden, these people were the biggest phonies of all
11. The school
12. James ____ committed suicide
13. Elevator operator who set Holden up with Sunny
14. Holden's transportation to NY
15. Author
16. Little Shirley ___; record Holden bought Phoebe
17. The ___ In The Rye
18. Lillian; DB's old girlfriend
19. Topic of the composition Holden wrote for Stradlater
20. Narrator; Holden

Catcher In The Rye Fill In The Blank 3 Answer Key

MORON	1. Holden calls people this when they do things that don't suit him
POEMS	2. Allie's glove had these written on it
FENCING	3. Holden returned to school with the ___ team
CAROUSEL	4. Holden watched Phoebe ride one
IMMATURE	5. An ___ man wants to die nobly for a cause.
GALLAGHER	6. Checker-playing neighbor friend of Holden: Jane ___
ERNIE	7. Holden lied to his mother on the train
MUSEUM	8. Holden liked it because everything there stayed put
STRADLATER	9. Holden's roommate who was good-looking but conceited
ACTORS	10. According to Holden, these people were the biggest phonies of all
PENCEY	11. The school
CASTLE	12. James ___ committed suicide
MAURICE	13. Elevator operator who set Holden up with Sunny
TRAIN	14. Holden's transportation to NY
SALINGER	15. Author
BEANS	16. Little Shirley ___; record Holden bought Phoebe
CATCHER	17. The ___ In The Rye
SIMMONS	18. Lillian; DB's old girlfriend
GLOVE	19. Topic of the composition Holden wrote for Stradlater
CAULFIELD	20. Narrator; Holden

Catcher In The Rye Fill In The Blank 4

_____

1. Allie's glove had these written on it
2. An ___ man wants to die nobly for a cause.
3. The prostitute
4. Holden lied to his mother on the train
5. Narrator; Holden
6. Holden chatted with them at the sandwich bar
7. Holden was kicked out of Pencey because he ___
8. Season to be jolly
9. Topic of the composition Holden wrote for Stradlater
10. Holden's dead brother
11. Stradlater gave Holden a bloody one
12. Phoebe packed hers so she could go with Holden
13. Roomed next to Holden at Pencey
14. Holden's sister
15. Checker-playing neighbor friend of Holden: Jane ___
16. Little Shirley ___; record Holden bought Phoebe
17. James ___ committed suicide
18. Student at Whooton; had a drink with Holden
19. Holden watched Phoebe ride one
20. Holden's roommate who was good-looking but conceited

Catcher In The Rye Fill In The Blank 4 Answer Key

POEMS	1. Allie's glove had these written on it
IMMATURE	2. An ___ man wants to die nobly for a cause.
SUNNY	3. The prostitute
ERNIE	4. Holden lied to his mother on the train
CAULFIELD	5. Narrator; Holden
NUNS	6. Holden chatted with them at the sandwich bar
FAILED	7. Holden was kicked out of Pencey because he ___
CHRISTMAS	8. Season to be jolly
GLOVE	9. Topic of the composition Holden wrote for Stradlater
ALLIE	10. Holden's dead brother
NOSE	11. Stradlater gave Holden a bloody one
BAGS	12. Phoebe packed hers so she could go with Holden
ACKLEY	13. Roomed next to Holden at Pencey
PHOEBE	14. Holden's sister
GALLAGHER	15. Checker-playing neighbor friend of Holden: Jane ___
BEANS	16. Little Shirley ___; record Holden bought Phoebe
CASTLE	17. James ___ committed suicide
LUCE	18. Student at Whooton; had a drink with Holden
CAROUSEL	19. Holden watched Phoebe ride one
STRADLATER	20. Holden's roommate who was good-looking but conceited

Catcher In The Rye Matching 1

___ 1. ANTOLINI   A. The ___ In The Rye
___ 2. MAURICE   B. Holden returned to school with the ___ team
___ 3. LAVENDER   C. An ___ man wants to die nobly for a cause.
___ 4. CASTLE   D. English teacher
___ 5. PHOEBE   E. Student at Whooton; had a drink with Holden
___ 6. ERNIE   F. The school
___ 7. SPENCER   G. James ___ committed suicide
___ 8. POEMS   H. Holden liked it because everything there stayed put
___ 9. IMMATURE   I. Season to be jolly
___10. CHRISTMAS   J. Holden lied to his mother on the train
___11. SIMMONS   K. Holden's theater date
___12. MUSEUM   L. Lillian; DB's old girlfriend
___13. FAILED   M. Holden calls people this when they do things that don't suit him
___14. PENCEY   N. Holden's roommate who was good-looking but conceited
___15. GLOVE   O. Holden was kicked out of Pencey because he ___
___16. MORON   P. Topic of the composition Holden wrote for Stradlater
___17. GALLAGHER   Q. Elevator operator who set Holden up with Sunny
___18. FENCING   R. History teacher
___19. SALINGER   S. Checker-playing neighbor friend of Holden: Jane ___
___20. CATCHER   T. Narrator; Holden
___21. LUCE   U. Author
___22. SALLY   V. Phoebe packed hers so she could go with Holden
___23. CAULFIELD   W. Holden's sister
___24. STRADLATER   X. Bernice and friends danced with Holden at the ___ Room
___25. BAGS   Y. Allie's glove had these written on it

Catcher In The Rye Matching 1 Answer Key

D - 1. ANTOLINI   A. The ___ In The Rye
Q - 2. MAURICE   B. Holden returned to school with the ___ team
X - 3. LAVENDER   C. An ___ man wants to die nobly for a cause.
G - 4. CASTLE   D. English teacher
W - 5. PHOEBE   E. Student at Whooton; had a drink with Holden
J - 6. ERNIE   F. The school
R - 7. SPENCER   G. James ___ committed suicide
Y - 8. POEMS   H. Holden liked it because everything there stayed put
C - 9. IMMATURE   I. Season to be jolly
I - 10. CHRISTMAS   J. Holden lied to his mother on the train
L - 11. SIMMONS   K. Holden's theater date
H - 12. MUSEUM   L. Lillian; DB's old girlfriend
O - 13. FAILED   M. Holden calls people this when they do things that don't suit him
F - 14. PENCEY   N. Holden's roommate who was good-looking but conceited
P - 15. GLOVE   O. Holden was kicked out of Pencey because he ___
M - 16. MORON   P. Topic of the composition Holden wrote for Stradlater
S - 17. GALLAGHER   Q. Elevator operator who set Holden up with Sunny
B - 18. FENCING   R. History teacher
U - 19. SALINGER   S. Checker-playing neighbor friend of Holden: Jane ___
A - 20. CATCHER   T. Narrator; Holden
E - 21. LUCE   U. Author
K - 22. SALLY   V. Phoebe packed hers so she could go with Holden
T - 23. CAULFIELD   W. Holden's sister
N - 24. STRADLATER   X. Bernice and friends danced with Holden at the ___ Room
V - 25. BAGS   Y. Allie's glove had these written on it

Catcher In The Rye Matching 2

___ 1. FAILED
___ 2. PENCEY
___ 3. IMMATURE
___ 4. SALINGER
___ 5. SUNNY
___ 6. SALLY
___ 7. BAGS
___ 8. POEMS
___ 9. LUCE
___ 10. MAURICE
___ 11. ALLIE
___ 12. CATCHER
___ 13. FENCING
___ 14. CHRISTMAS
___ 15. CAULFIELD
___ 16. CAROUSEL
___ 17. ERNIE
___ 18. CASTLE
___ 19. MUSEUM
___ 20. ANTOLINI
___ 21. GALLAGHER
___ 22. ACKLEY
___ 23. SPENCER
___ 24. ACTORS
___ 25. TRAIN

A. Allie's glove had these written on it
B. James ____ committed suicide
C. Holden's theater date
D. An ____ man wants to die nobly for a cause.
E. Holden was kicked out of Pencey because he ___
F. Holden liked it because everything there stayed put
G. Student at Whooton; had a drink with Holden
H. Holden's dead brother
I. English teacher
J. Holden's transportation to NY
K. Season to be jolly
L. Elevator operator who set Holden up with Sunny
M. Author
N. Phoebe packed hers so she could go with Holden
O. Holden lied to his mother on the train
P. Roomed next to Holden at Pencey
Q. The school
R. Holden watched Phoebe ride one
S. According to Holden, these people were the biggest phonies of all
T. History teacher
U. The ___ In The Rye
V. The prostitute
W. Narrator; Holden
X. Holden returned to school with the ___ team
Y. Checker-playing neighbor friend of Holden: Jane ___

Catcher In The Rye Matching 2 Answer Key

E - 1. FAILED   A. Allie's glove had these written on it
Q - 2. PENCEY   B. James ____ committed suicide
D - 3. IMMATURE   C. Holden's theater date
M - 4. SALINGER   D. An ___ man wants to die nobly for a cause.
V - 5. SUNNY   E. Holden was kicked out of Pencey because he ___
C - 6. SALLY   F. Holden liked it because everything there stayed put
N - 7. BAGS   G. Student at Whooton; had a drink with Holden
A - 8. POEMS   H. Holden's dead brother
G - 9. LUCE   I. English teacher
L - 10. MAURICE   J. Holden's transportation to NY
H - 11. ALLIE   K. Season to be jolly
U - 12. CATCHER   L. Elevator operator who set Holden up with Sunny
X - 13. FENCING   M. Author
K - 14. CHRISTMAS   N. Phoebe packed hers so she could go with Holden
W - 15. CAULFIELD   O. Holden lied to his mother on the train
R - 16. CAROUSEL   P. Roomed next to Holden at Pencey
O - 17. ERNIE   Q. The school
B - 18. CASTLE   R. Holden watched Phoebe ride one
F - 19. MUSEUM   S. According to Holden, these people were the biggest phonies of all
I - 20. ANTOLINI   T. History teacher
Y - 21. GALLAGHER   U. The ___ In The Rye
P - 22. ACKLEY   V. The prostitute
T - 23. SPENCER   W. Narrator; Holden
S - 24. ACTORS   X. Holden returned to school with the ___ team
J - 25. TRAIN   Y. Checker-playing neighbor friend of Holden: Jane ___

Catcher In The Rye Matching 3

___ 1. ERNIE   A. The ___ In The Rye

___ 2. ACTORS   B. Topic of the composition Holden wrote for Stradlater

___ 3. SPENCER   C. History teacher

___ 4. CASTLE   D. According to Holden, these people were the biggest phonies of all

___ 5. TRAIN   E. An ___ man wants to die nobly for a cause.

___ 6. PHOEBE   F. Little Shirley ___; record Holden bought Phoebe

___ 7. MAURICE   G. English teacher

___ 8. SUNNY   H. Holden's roommate who was good-looking but conceited

___ 9. MORON   I. Author

___ 10. CAULFIELD   J. Holden watched Phoebe ride one

___ 11. BEANS   K. Holden calls people this when they do things that don't suit him

___ 12. ANTOLINI   L. Holden's dead brother

___ 13. STRADLATER   M. James ___ committed suicide

___ 14. GLOVE   N. Holden's sister

___ 15. NUNS   O. Checker-playing neighbor friend of Holden: Jane ___

___ 16. SALLY   P. Holden's transportation to NY

___ 17. NOSE   Q. Holden chatted with them at the sandwich bar

___ 18. SALINGER   R. Elevator operator who set Holden up with Sunny

___ 19. CAROUSEL   S. Holden was kicked out of Pencey because he ___

___ 20. GALLAGHER   T. The prostitute

___ 21. CATCHER   U. Lillian; DB's old girlfriend

___ 22. IMMATURE   V. Holden's theater date

___ 23. SIMMONS   W. Narrator; Holden

___ 24. ALLIE   X. Holden lied to his mother on the train

___ 25. FAILED   Y. Stradlater gave Holden a bloody one

Catcher In The Rye Matching 3 Answer Key

X - 1. ERNIE	A. The ___ In The Rye
D - 2. ACTORS	B. Topic of the composition Holden wrote for Stradlater
C - 3. SPENCER	C. History teacher
M - 4. CASTLE	D. According to Holden, these people were the biggest phonies of all
P - 5. TRAIN	E. An ___ man wants to die nobly for a cause.
N - 6. PHOEBE	F. Little Shirley ___; record Holden bought Phoebe
R - 7. MAURICE	G. English teacher
T - 8. SUNNY	H. Holden's roommate who was good-looking but conceited
K - 9. MORON	I. Author
W - 10. CAULFIELD	J. Holden watched Phoebe ride one
F - 11. BEANS	K. Holden calls people this when they do things that don't suit him
G - 12. ANTOLINI	L. Holden's dead brother
H - 13. STRADLATER	M. James ___ committed suicide
B - 14. GLOVE	N. Holden's sister
Q - 15. NUNS	O. Checker-playing neighbor friend of Holden: Jane ___
V - 16. SALLY	P. Holden's transportation to NY
Y - 17. NOSE	Q. Holden chatted with them at the sandwich bar
I - 18. SALINGER	R. Elevator operator who set Holden up with Sunny
J - 19. CAROUSEL	S. Holden was kicked out of Pencey because he ___
O - 20. GALLAGHER	T. The prostitute
A - 21. CATCHER	U. Lillian; DB's old girlfriend
E - 22. IMMATURE	V. Holden's theater date
U - 23. SIMMONS	W. Narrator; Holden
L - 24. ALLIE	X. Holden lied to his mother on the train
S - 25. FAILED	Y. Stradlater gave Holden a bloody one

Catcher In The Rye Matching 4

___ 1. NUNS
___ 2. NOSE
___ 3. PHOEBE
___ 4. SALINGER
___ 5. GLOVE
___ 6. PENCEY
___ 7. CATCHER
___ 8. LUCE
___ 9. ALLIE
___ 10. FENCING
___ 11. ERNIE
___ 12. FAILED
___ 13. ACTORS
___ 14. LAVENDER
___ 15. POEMS
___ 16. SALLY
___ 17. BEANS
___ 18. CAROUSEL
___ 19. CASTLE
___ 20. IMMATURE
___ 21. ANTOLINI
___ 22. SIMMONS
___ 23. TRAIN
___ 24. STRADLATER
___ 25. SUNNY

A. The school
B. Lillian; DB's old girlfriend
C. Topic of the composition Holden wrote for Stradlater
D. An ___ man wants to die nobly for a cause.
E. Holden returned to school with the ___ team
F. English teacher
G. Little Shirley ___; record Holden bought Phoebe
H. Holden's theater date
I. Holden was kicked out of Pencey because he ___
J. Allie's glove had these written on it
K. Holden lied to his mother on the train
L. Holden watched Phoebe ride one
M. Holden's roommate who was good-looking but conceited
N. Author
O. Holden's dead brother
P. Student at Whooton; had a drink with Holden
Q. Bernice and friends danced with Holden at the ___ Room
R. The prostitute
S. James ___ committed suicide
T. Holden chatted with them at the sandwich bar
U. According to Holden, these people were the biggest phonies of all
V. Holden's transportation to NY
W. Stradlater gave Holden a bloody one
X. Holden's sister
Y. The ___ In The Rye

Catcher In The Rye Matching 4 Answer Key

T - 1. NUNS   A. The school
W - 2. NOSE   B. Lillian; DB's old girlfriend
X - 3. PHOEBE   C. Topic of the composition Holden wrote for Stradlater
N - 4. SALINGER   D. An ___ man wants to die nobly for a cause.
C - 5. GLOVE   E. Holden returned to school with the ___ team
A - 6. PENCEY   F. English teacher
Y - 7. CATCHER   G. Little Shirley ___; record Holden bought Phoebe
P - 8. LUCE   H. Holden's theater date
O - 9. ALLIE   I. Holden was kicked out of Pencey because he ___
E - 10. FENCING   J. Allie's glove had these written on it
K - 11. ERNIE   K. Holden lied to his mother on the train
I - 12. FAILED   L. Holden watched Phoebe ride one
U - 13. ACTORS   M. Holden's roommate who was good-looking but conceited
Q - 14. LAVENDER   N. Author
J - 15. POEMS   O. Holden's dead brother
H - 16. SALLY   P. Student at Whooton; had a drink with Holden
G - 17. BEANS   Q. Bernice and friends danced with Holden at the ___ Room
L - 18. CAROUSEL   R. The prostitute
S - 19. CASTLE   S. James ___ committed suicide
D - 20. IMMATURE   T. Holden chatted with them at the sandwich bar
F - 21. ANTOLINI   U. According to Holden, these people were the biggest phonies of all
B - 22. SIMMONS   V. Holden's transportation to NY
V - 23. TRAIN   W. Stradlater gave Holden a bloody one
M - 24. STRADLATER   X. Holden's sister
R - 25. SUNNY   Y. The ___ In The Rye

Catcher In The Rye Magic Squares 1

Match the definition with the vocabulary word. Put your answers in the magic squares below. When your answers are correct, all columns and rows will add to the same number.

A. SALINGER
B. NOSE
C. GALLAGHER
D. GLOVE
E. ANTOLINI
F. ACKLEY
G. PHOEBE
H. IMMATURE
I. LAVENDER
J. SALLY
K. ERNIE
L. MUSEUM
M. PENCEY
N. CAULFIELD
O. MORON
P. LUCE

1. An ___ man wants to die nobly for a cause.
2. The school
3. Stradlater gave Holden a bloody one
4. Holden lied to his mother on the train
5. Holden's theater date
6. Checker-playing neighbor friend of Holden: Jane ___
7. Student at Whooton; had a drink with Holden
8. English teacher
9. Holden calls people this when they do things that don't suit him
10. Roomed next to Holden at Pencey
11. Bernice and friends danced with Holden at the ___ Room
12. Topic of the composition Holden wrote for Stradlater
13. Author
14. Holden liked it because everything there stayed put
15. Holden's sister
16. Narrator; Holden

A=	B=	C=	D=
E=	F=	G=	H=
I=	J=	K=	L=
M=	N=	O=	P=

Catcher In The Rye Magic Squares 1 Answer Key

Match the definition with the vocabulary word. Put your answers in the magic squares below. When your answers are correct, all columns and rows will add to the same number.

A. SALINGER
B. NOSE
C. GALLAGHER
D. GLOVE
E. ANTOLINI
F. ACKLEY
G. PHOEBE
H. IMMATURE
I. LAVENDER
J. SALLY
K. ERNIE
L. MUSEUM
M. PENCEY
N. CAULFIELD
O. MORON
P. LUCE

1. An ___ man wants to die nobly for a cause.
2. The school
3. Stradlater gave Holden a bloody one
4. Holden lied to his mother on the train
5. Holden's theater date
6. Checker-playing neighbor friend of Holden: Jane ___
7. Student at Whooton; had a drink with Holden
8. English teacher
9. Holden calls people this when they do things that don't suit him
10. Roomed next to Holden at Pencey
11. Bernice and friends danced with Holden at the ___ Room
12. Topic of the composition Holden wrote for Stradlater
13. Author
14. Holden liked it because everything there stayed put
15. Holden's sister
16. Narrator; Holden

A=13	B=3	C=6	D=12
E=8	F=10	G=15	H=1
I=11	J=5	K=4	L=14
M=2	N=16	O=9	P=7

Catcher In The Rye Magic Squares 2

Match the definition with the vocabulary word. Put your answers in the magic squares below. When your answers are correct, all columns and rows will add to the same number.

A. LUCE
B. ANTOLINI
C. SUNNY
D. NOSE
E. IMMATURE
F. LAVENDER
G. CASTLE
H. FENCING
I. GALLAGHER
J. SALLY
K. MUSEUM
L. ACKLEY
M. BAGS
N. ERNIE
O. PENCEY
P. FAILED

1. Student at Whooton; had a drink with Holden
2. Holden lied to his mother on the train
3. Holden's theater date
4. An ___ man wants to die nobly for a cause.
5. James ___ committed suicide
6. Roomed next to Holden at Pencey
7. Holden was kicked out of Pencey because he ___
8. The prostitute
9. The school
10. Stradlater gave Holden a bloody one
11. Holden returned to school with the ___ team
12. Holden liked it because everything there stayed put
13. Checker-playing neighbor friend of Holden: Jane ___
14. Bernice and friends danced with Holden at the ___ Room
15. English teacher
16. Phoebe packed hers so she could go with Holden

A=	B=	C=	D=
E=	F=	G=	H=
I=	J=	K=	L=
M=	N=	O=	P=

Catcher In The Rye Magic Squares 2 Answer Key

Match the definition with the vocabulary word. Put your answers in the magic squares below. When your answers are correct, all columns and rows will add to the same number.

A. LUCE
B. ANTOLINI
C. SUNNY
D. NOSE
E. IMMATURE
F. LAVENDER
G. CASTLE
H. FENCING
I. GALLAGHER
J. SALLY
K. MUSEUM
L. ACKLEY
M. BAGS
N. ERNIE
O. PENCEY
P. FAILED

1. Student at Whooton; had a drink with Holden
2. Holden lied to his mother on the train
3. Holden's theater date
4. An ___ man wants to die nobly for a cause.
5. James ____ committed suicide
6. Roomed next to Holden at Pencey
7. Holden was kicked out of Pencey because he ___
8. The prostitute
9. The school
10. Stradlater gave Holden a bloody one
11. Holden returned to school with the ___ team
12. Holden liked it because everything there stayed put
13. Checker-playing neighbor friend of Holden: Jane ___
14. Bernice and friends danced with Holden at the ___ Room
15. English teacher
16. Phoebe packed hers so she could go with Holden

A=1	B=15	C=8	D=10
E=4	F=14	G=5	H=11
I=13	J=3	K=12	L=6
M=16	N=2	O=9	P=7

Catcher In The Rye Magic Squares 3

Match the definition with the vocabulary word. Put your answers in the magic squares below. When your answers are correct, all columns and rows will add to the same number.

A. POEMS
B. BAGS
C. SALLY
D. MORON
E. GLOVE
F. LUCE
G. LAVENDER
H. SUNNY
I. ALLIE
J. CATCHER
K. IMMATURE
L. FAILED
M. NOSE
N. ACTORS
O. SPENCER
P. TRAIN

1. Student at Whooton; had a drink with Holden
2. Holden's dead brother
3. History teacher
4. Holden calls people this when they do things that don't suit him
5. Stradlater gave Holden a bloody one
6. Phoebe packed hers so she could go with Holden
7. The prostitute
8. An ___ man wants to die nobly for a cause.
9. Holden's theater date
10. Holden's transportation to NY
11. The ___ In The Rye
12. Topic of the composition Holden wrote for Stradlater
13. Holden was kicked out of Pencey because he ___
14. Bernice and friends danced with Holden at the ___ Room
15. Allie's glove had these written on it
16. According to Holden, these people were the biggest phonies of all

A=	B=	C=	D=
E=	F=	G=	H=
I=	J=	K=	L=
M=	N=	O=	P=

Catcher In The Rye Magic Squares 3 Answer Key

Match the definition with the vocabulary word. Put your answers in the magic squares below. When your answers are correct, all columns and rows will add to the same number.

A. POEMS
B. BAGS
C. SALLY
D. MORON
E. GLOVE
F. LUCE
G. LAVENDER
H. SUNNY
I. ALLIE
J. CATCHER
K. IMMATURE
L. FAILED
M. NOSE
N. ACTORS
O. SPENCER
P. TRAIN

1. Student at Whooton; had a drink with Holden
2. Holden's dead brother
3. History teacher
4. Holden calls people this when they do things that don't suit him
5. Stradlater gave Holden a bloody one
6. Phoebe packed hers so she could go with Holden
7. The prostitute
8. An ___ man wants to die nobly for a cause.
9. Holden's theater date
10. Holden's transportation to NY
11. The ___ In The Rye
12. Topic of the composition Holden wrote for Stradlater
13. Holden was kicked out of Pencey because he ___
14. Bernice and friends danced with Holden at the ___ Room
15. Allie's glove had these written on it
16. According to Holden, these people were the biggest phonies of all

A=15	B=6	C=9	D=4
E=12	F=1	G=14	H=7
I=2	J=11	K=8	L=13
M=5	N=16	O=3	P=10

Copyrighted

Catcher In The Rye Magic Squares 4

Match the definition with the vocabulary word. Put your answers in the magic squares below. When your answers are correct, all columns and rows will add to the same number.

A. SUNNY
B. ERNIE
C. FENCING
D. TRAIN
E. ACKLEY
F. MUSEUM
G. SALLY
H. SALINGER
I. GALLAGHER
J. ALLIE
K. CAROUSEL
L. BAGS
M. CHRISTMAS
N. MORON
O. BEANS
P. CAULFIELD

1. Little Shirley ___; record Holden bought Phoebe
2. Holden's transportation to NY
3. Holden's dead brother
4. Roomed next to Holden at Pencey
5. Checker-playing neighbor friend of Holden: Jane ___
6. Holden liked it because everything there stayed put
7. Narrator; Holden
8. Holden returned to school with the ___ team
9. Author
10. Holden watched Phoebe ride one
11. The prostitute
12. Holden calls people this when they do things that don't suit him
13. Holden lied to his mother on the train
14. Season to be jolly
15. Holden's theater date
16. Phoebe packed hers so she could go with Holden

A=	B=	C=	D=
E=	F=	G=	H=
I=	J=	K=	L=
M=	N=	O=	P=

Catcher In The Rye Magic Squares 4 Answer Key

Match the definition with the vocabulary word. Put your answers in the magic squares below. When your answers are correct, all columns and rows will add to the same number.

A. SUNNY
B. ERNIE
C. FENCING
D. TRAIN
E. ACKLEY
F. MUSEUM
G. SALLY
H. SALINGER
I. GALLAGHER
J. ALLIE
K. CAROUSEL
L. BAGS
M. CHRISTMAS
N. MORON
O. BEANS
P. CAULFIELD

1. Little Shirley ___; record Holden bought Phoebe
2. Holden's transportation to NY
3. Holden's dead brother
4. Roomed next to Holden at Pencey
5. Checker-playing neighbor friend of Holden: Jane ___
6. Holden liked it because everything there stayed put
7. Narrator; Holden
8. Holden returned to school with the ___ team
9. Author
10. Holden watched Phoebe ride one
11. The prostitute
12. Holden calls people this when they do things that don't suit him
13. Holden lied to his mother on the train
14. Season to be jolly
15. Holden's theater date
16. Phoebe packed hers so she could go with Holden

A=11	B=13	C=8	D=2
E=4	F=6	G=15	H=9
I=5	J=3	K=10	L=16
M=14	N=12	O=1	P=7

Catcher In The Rye Word Search 1

Words are placed backwards, forward, diagonally, up and down. Clues listed below can help you find the words. Circle the hidden vocabulary words in the maze.

```
Y B C C S C G R X F Z H P T F Y I B L Z
X P V A K U C L R W E G Y T W G N Y A V
J B L R U M N C O K Q N W R C E I E V R
M L M O N L R N S V X V C A C H L C E F
Y E C U L P F N Y V E R N I E S O N N K
J G N S S O A I F S J Y R N N J T E D N
Y S A E G E P F E G R U P H J G N P E W
A K N L B M U H S L A A J N F V A C R C
L C R J L S Z M O M D C A T C H E R J N
L B T F S A X Y B E R K Q E Y R S M T P
I X V O T N G A X Z B L Z L U S P O P C
E V Z S R R G H D H T E S T B S E R Z Y
G Y D I A S Z V E Y W Y A S L G N O R W
N G X M D M D D L R H M M A L W C N K M
Y P F M L Q S D I W M N T C J C E S L Y
N W K O A L B H A I T Q S W V C R S Y B
D J N N T M M G F K T P I Y R B D N L F
G G Y S E B X V K Q J H R H S S X X Y F
M B Y R R N F P V V N Y H J L W R T X Z
S A L I N G E R F P X N C Y B T K B L V
```

According to Holden, these people were the biggest phonies of all (6)
Allie's glove had these written on it (5)
An ___ man wants to die nobly for a cause. (8)
Author (8)
Bernice and friends danced with Holden at the ___ Room (8)
Checker-playing neighbor friend of Holden: Jane ___ (9)
Elevator operator who set Holden up with Sunny (7)
English teacher (8)
History teacher (7)
Holden calls people this when they do things that don't suit him (5)
Holden chatted with them at the sandwich bar (4)
Holden lied to his mother on the train (5)
Holden liked it because everything there stayed put (6)
Holden returned to school with the ___ team (7)
Holden was kicked out of Pencey because he ___ (6)
Holden watched Phoebe ride one (8)

Holden's dead brother (5)
Holden's roommate who was good-looking but conceited (10)
Holden's sister (6)
Holden's theater date (5)
Holden's transportation to NY (5)
James ___ committed suicide (6)
Lillian; DB's old girlfriend (7)
Little Shirley ___; record Holden bought Phoebe (5)
Narrator; Holden (9)
Phoebe packed hers so she could go with Holden (4)
Roomed next to Holden at Pencey (6)
Season to be jolly (9)
Stradlater gave Holden a bloody one (4)
Student at Whooton; had a drink with Holden (4)
The ___ In The Rye (7)
The prostitute (5)
The school (6)
Topic of the composition Holden wrote for Stradlater (5)

Catcher In The Rye Word Search 1 Answer Key

Words are placed backwards, forward, diagonally, up and down. Clues listed below can help you find the words. Circle the hidden vocabulary words in the maze.

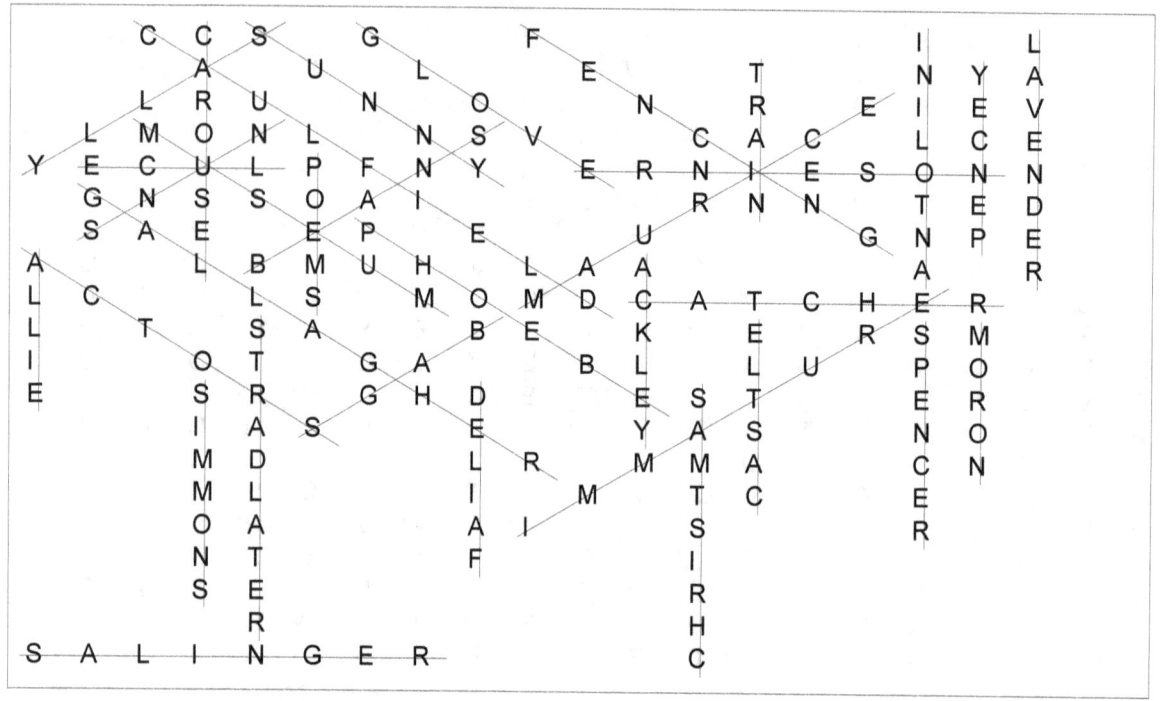

According to Holden, these people were the biggest phonies of all (6)
Allie's glove had these written on it (5)
An ___ man wants to die nobly for a cause. (8)
Author (8)
Bernice and friends danced with Holden at the ___ Room (8)
Checker-playing neighbor friend of Holden: Jane ___ (9)
Elevator operator who set Holden up with Sunny (7)
English teacher (8)
History teacher (7)
Holden calls people this when they do things that don't suit him (5)
Holden chatted with them at the sandwich bar (4)
Holden lied to his mother on the train (5)
Holden liked it because everything there stayed put (6)
Holden returned to school with the ___ team (7)
Holden was kicked out of Pencey because he ___ (6)
Holden watched Phoebe ride one (8)

Holden's dead brother (5)
Holden's roommate who was good-looking but conceited (10)
Holden's sister (6)
Holden's theater date (5)
Holden's transportation to NY (5)
James ___ committed suicide (6)
Lillian; DB's old girlfriend (7)
Little Shirley ___; record Holden bought Phoebe (5)
Narrator; Holden (9)
Phoebe packed hers so she could go with Holden (4)
Roomed next to Holden at Pencey (6)
Season to be jolly (9)
Stradlater gave Holden a bloody one (4)
Student at Whooton; had a drink with Holden (4)
The ___ In The Rye (7)
The prostitute (5)
The school (6)
Topic of the composition Holden wrote for Stradlater (5)

30
Copyrighted

Catcher In The Rye Word Search 2

Words are placed backwards, forward, diagonally, up and down. Clues listed below can help you find the words. Circle the hidden vocabulary words in the maze.

```
G S Z K K X P W Q S S E G J N N W F C B
L H B H C O Y M S N H W R X J N B E A X
O N A P E A W J C O T V Q N C O M N U W
V P G M E D R E T M R P N N I S R C L F
E M S I N S R O M M A U R I C E S I F M
D X L H X U E T U I I B P A G N N N I W
B L H R T S C D S S N Z T N U X A G E Q
A X L A W A N J E N E C I N C J E S L S
H Z M S T L E N U J H L K H P A B K D M
C M L V R L P T M E A G T G S E S D S K
I L U C E Y S N R S R O T C A S N T K P
A Z L Q H N M L N B Z N V C L B R C L Z
X N S X G N Q C A Y N N J G G A P H E E
T T T B A U B G P V Q F M L D F H R D Y
M L H O L S A C K L E Y H L S D O I B T
C O P M L R B V Z Z J N A D E C E S S T
Z Q R B A I S P V W W T D L K G B T H M
N S Z O G T N R C Q E F I E P T E M F X
X Y H V N L D I H R Z A L H R F C A X Y
H K Q Z W D F Q F B F F F S P H W S T T
```

According to Holden, these people were the biggest phonies of all (6)
Allie's glove had these written on it (5)
An ___ man wants to die nobly for a cause. (8)
Author (8)
Bernice and friends danced with Holden at the ___ Room (8)
Checker-playing neighbor friend of Holden: Jane ___ (9)
Elevator operator who set Holden up with Sunny (7)
English teacher (8)
History teacher (7)
Holden calls people this when they do things that don't suit him (5)
Holden chatted with them at the sandwich bar (4)
Holden lied to his mother on the train (5)
Holden liked it because everything there stayed put (6)
Holden returned to school with the ___ team (7)
Holden was kicked out of Pencey because he ___ (6)
Holden watched Phoebe ride one (8)

Holden's dead brother (5)
Holden's roommate who was good-looking but conceited (10)
Holden's sister (6)
Holden's theater date (5)
Holden's transportation to NY (5)
James ___ committed suicide (6)
Lillian; DB's old girlfriend (7)
Little Shirley ___; record Holden bought Phoebe (5)
Narrator; Holden (9)
Phoebe packed hers so she could go with Holden (4)
Roomed next to Holden at Pencey (6)
Season to be jolly (9)
Stradlater gave Holden a bloody one (4)
Student at Whooton; had a drink with Holden (4)
The ___ In The Rye (7)
The prostitute (5)
The school (6)
Topic of the composition Holden wrote for Stradlater (5)

Catcher In The Rye Word Search 2 Answer Key

Words are placed backwards, forward, diagonally, up and down. Clues listed below can help you find the words. Circle the hidden vocabulary words in the maze.

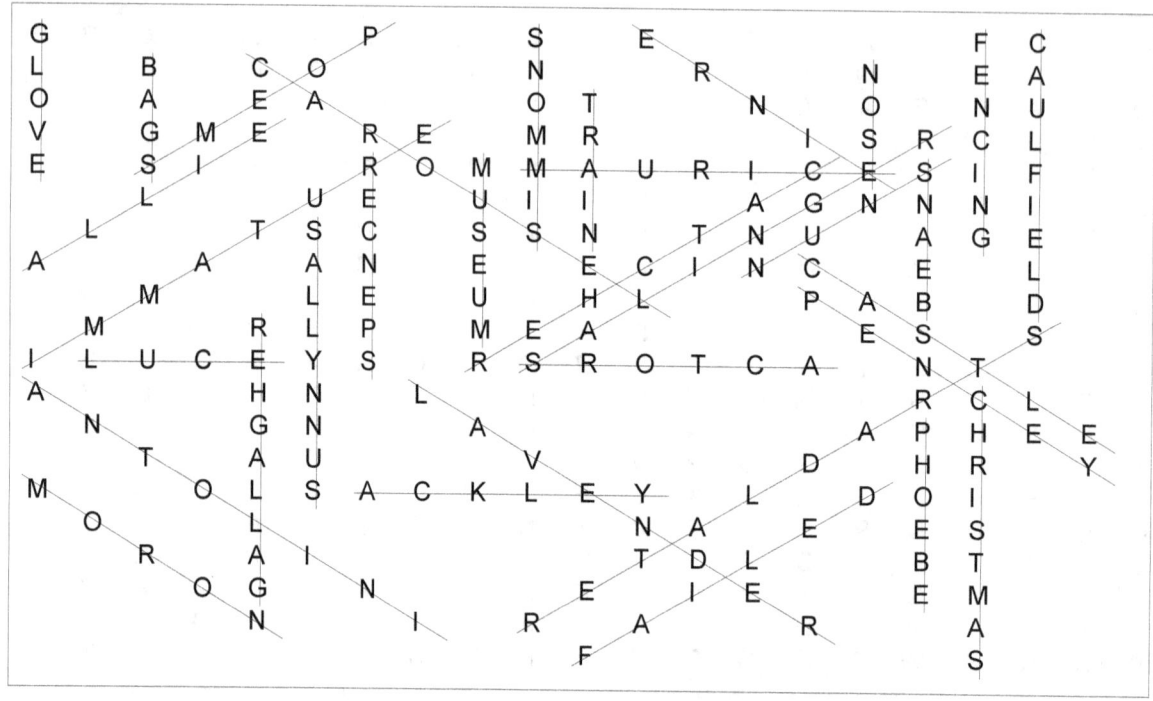

According to Holden, these people were the biggest phonies of all (6)
Allie's glove had these written on it (5)
An ___ man wants to die nobly for a cause. (8)
Author (8)
Bernice and friends danced with Holden at the ___ Room (8)
Checker-playing neighbor friend of Holden: Jane ___ (9)
Elevator operator who set Holden up with Sunny (7)
English teacher (8)
History teacher (7)
Holden calls people this when they do things that don't suit him (5)
Holden chatted with them at the sandwich bar (4)
Holden lied to his mother on the train (5)
Holden liked it because everything there stayed put (6)
Holden returned to school with the ___ team (7)
Holden was kicked out of Pencey because he ___ (6)
Holden watched Phoebe ride one (8)

Holden's dead brother (5)
Holden's roommate who was good-looking but conceited (10)
Holden's sister (6)
Holden's theater date (5)
Holden's transportation to NY (5)
James ____ committed suicide (6)
Lillian; DB's old girlfriend (7)
Little Shirley ___; record Holden bought Phoebe (5)
Narrator; Holden (9)
Phoebe packed hers so she could go with Holden (4)
Roomed next to Holden at Pencey (6)
Season to be jolly (9)
Stradlater gave Holden a bloody one (4)
Student at Whooton; had a drink with Holden (4)
The ___ In The Rye (7)
The prostitute (5)
The school (6)
Topic of the composition Holden wrote for Stradlater (5)

Catcher In The Rye Word Search 3

Words are placed backwards, forward, diagonally, up and down. Words listed below are included in the maze. Circle the hidden vocabulary words in the maze.

```
A C T O R S P N G N U N S G T B V S E S
N M Q T R L S N G S S C P L P F E I T W
T L R J E F I L T M L A E M W N L A T Q
O X K Q G C K Y E V A U N N A L X Y N F
L R R G N O R O M C V L C S A U H Q R S
I M D E I N P L S X E F E Z C S R M J J
N B F W L A Y Z R V N I R T M F V I F Q
I J J M A Q C G Q W D E G P Z K C L C Y
P M U E S U M K G C E L T S H K T Q F E
F E J F Y T C C L I R D W T K O X M A Q
P P N B H K C S N E Y Z R B D P E Y I Y
D N V C M V M R I K Y Y L L Z P M B L G
P W S I E W E S A M T S I R H C C W E A
P T T S M Y M W T B M G M T L A P G D L
Y G C B V M Y B L Q E O W S R J Y S L L
S V M Q H H A Q K L R M N O S L N W F A
L T Z X N J S T T P B I U S L V N O S G
D Q Y W C F G S U V A S P U N N U S S H
S T R A D L A T E R E H C T A C S P X E
G L O V E C B M T L E E S A L L Y S F R
```

ACKLEY	CAULFIELD	LUCE	SALINGER
ACTORS	CHRISTMAS	MAURICE	SALLY
ALLIE	ERNIE	MORON	SIMMONS
ANTOLINI	FAILED	MUSEUM	SPENCER
BAGS	FENCING	NOSE	STRADLATER
BEANS	GALLAGHER	NUNS	SUNNY
CAROUSEL	GLOVE	PENCEY	TRAIN
CASTLE	IMMATURE	PHOEBE	
CATCHER	LAVENDER	POEMS	

Catcher In The Rye Word Search 3 Answer Key

Words are placed backwards, forward, diagonally, up and down. Words listed below are included in the maze. Circle the hidden vocabulary words in the maze.

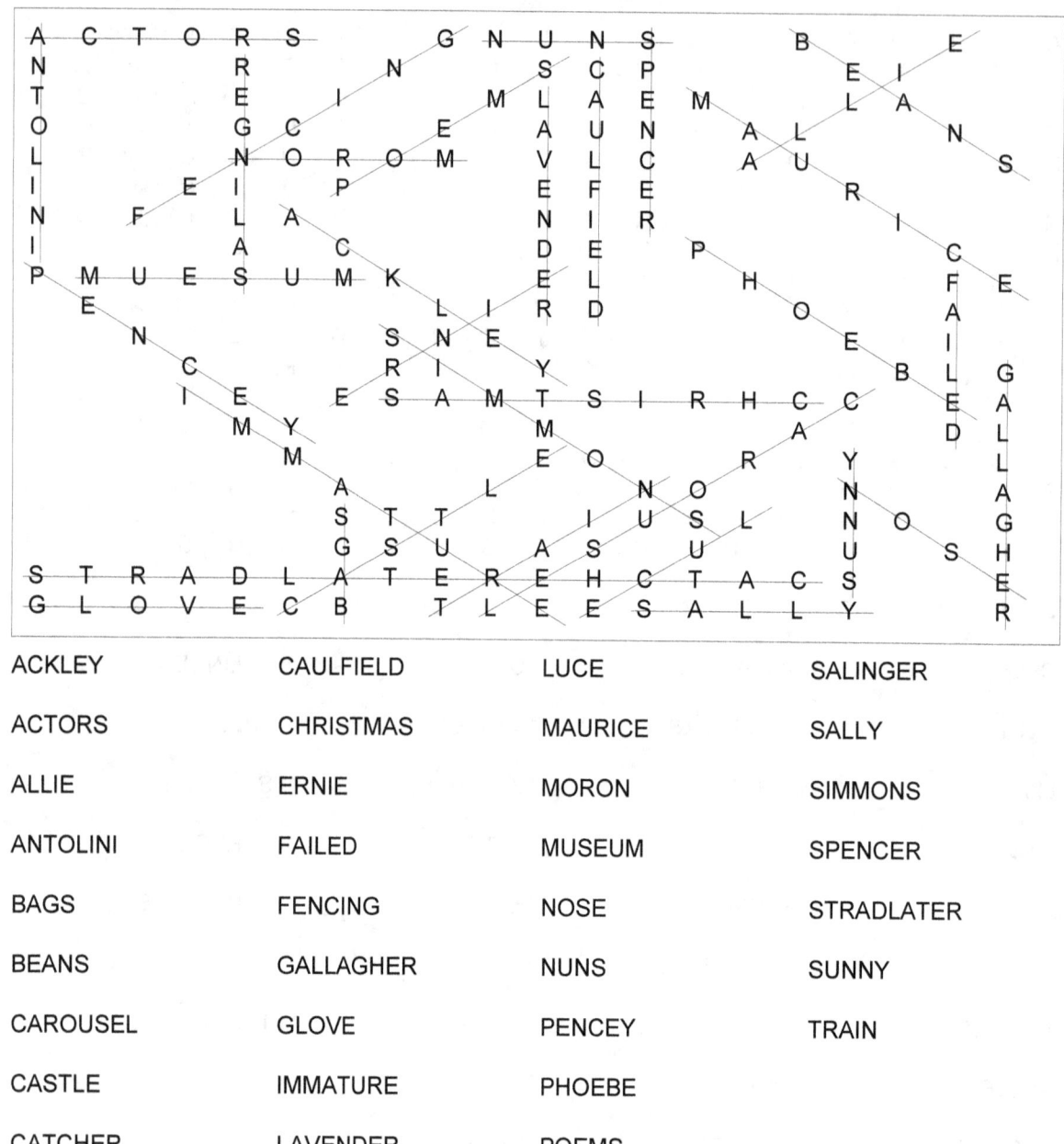

ACKLEY	CAULFIELD	LUCE	SALINGER
ACTORS	CHRISTMAS	MAURICE	SALLY
ALLIE	ERNIE	MORON	SIMMONS
ANTOLINI	FAILED	MUSEUM	SPENCER
BAGS	FENCING	NOSE	STRADLATER
BEANS	GALLAGHER	NUNS	SUNNY
CAROUSEL	GLOVE	PENCEY	TRAIN
CASTLE	IMMATURE	PHOEBE	
CATCHER	LAVENDER	POEMS	

Catcher In The Rye Word Search 4

Words are placed backwards, forward, diagonally, up and down. Words listed below are included in the maze. Circle the hidden vocabulary words in the maze.

```
B N O S E T R A I N U N S P E N C E R Y
A E H H M L J C M Q Q D C H D W B B L K
G R A D Y G F Y G V D L K E X P Q E K R
S U Z N B S S C K G D E L X W F V O G X
D T K C S G X R R G N I C N E F J H D V
M A H Q W M S E P L A F N Z L L B P Z V
L M J P Z B G T B F L L Y G C K P N K
Q M G Z H N H J R K W U Z Q B J H F F K
L I J P I K Z C S A B A H S Z L F M H D
W T M L S X R J C Y D C Z V I H Y R G N
R C A T C H E R B Y Y L M S R M P K K C
B S Q Q Y T C P T Y F L A O X K M L X S
C A R O U S E L P P W U F T R Z C O T Y
G A L L A G H E R J O C W P E O D M N F
P R E D N E V A L L I E G Y E R N M F S
F Y Y E L K C A P H L H M L T N U N A F
P A N T O L I N I T S T S S O E C L J H
F Q N J J L H M S Q H P N L S V L E R G
M A U R I C E A E R N I E U S Y E G Y L
B M S R O T C A Q R S A M T S I R H C N
```

ACKLEY   CAULFIELD   LUCE   SALINGER

ACTORS   CHRISTMAS   MAURICE   SALLY

ALLIE   ERNIE   MORON   SIMMONS

ANTOLINI   FAILED   MUSEUM   SPENCER

BAGS   FENCING   NOSE   STRADLATER

BEANS   GALLAGHER   NUNS   SUNNY

CAROUSEL   GLOVE   PENCEY   TRAIN

CASTLE   IMMATURE   PHOEBE

CATCHER   LAVENDER   POEMS

Catcher In The Rye Word Search 4 Answer Key

Words are placed backwards, forward, diagonally, up and down. Words listed below are included in the maze. Circle the hidden vocabulary words in the maze.

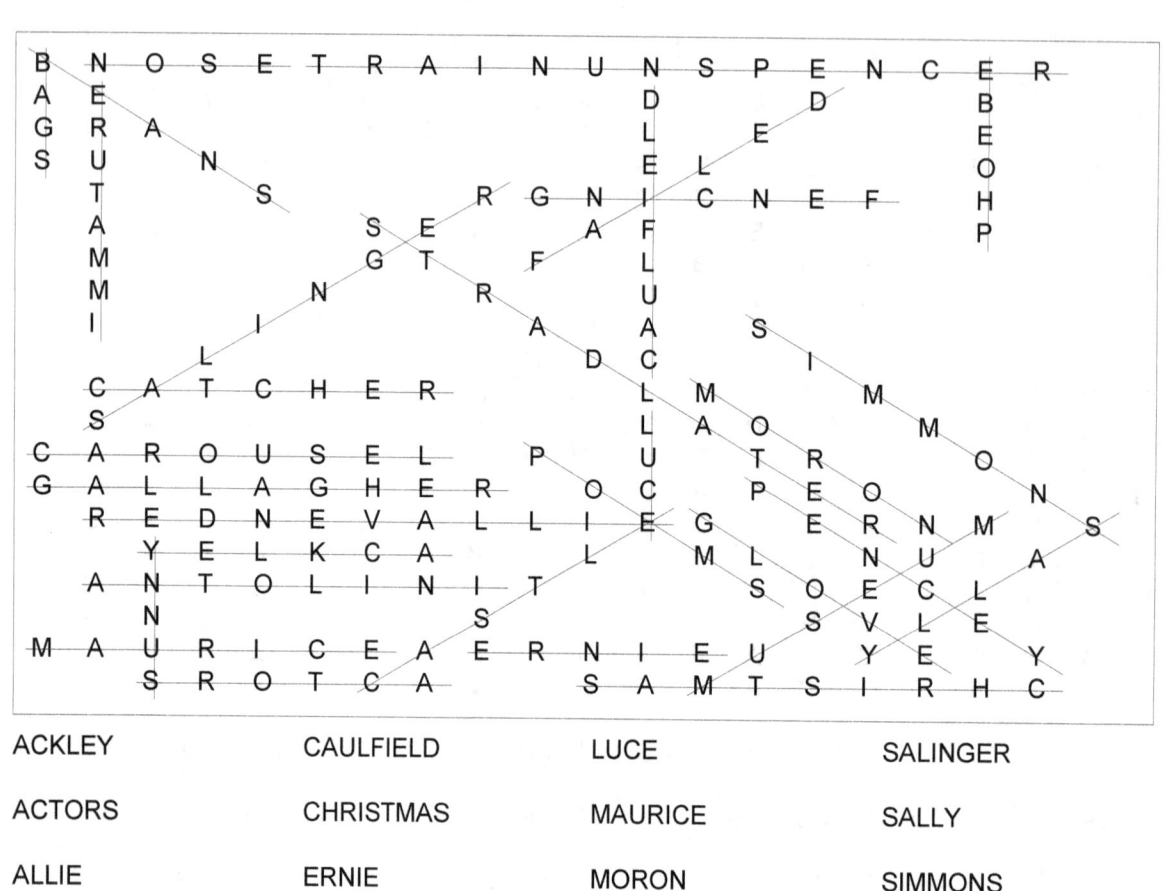

ACKLEY	CAULFIELD	LUCE	SALINGER
ACTORS	CHRISTMAS	MAURICE	SALLY
ALLIE	ERNIE	MORON	SIMMONS
ANTOLINI	FAILED	MUSEUM	SPENCER
BAGS	FENCING	NOSE	STRADLATER
BEANS	GALLAGHER	NUNS	SUNNY
CAROUSEL	GLOVE	PENCEY	TRAIN
CASTLE	IMMATURE	PHOEBE	
CATCHER	LAVENDER	POEMS	

Catcher In The Rye Crossword 1

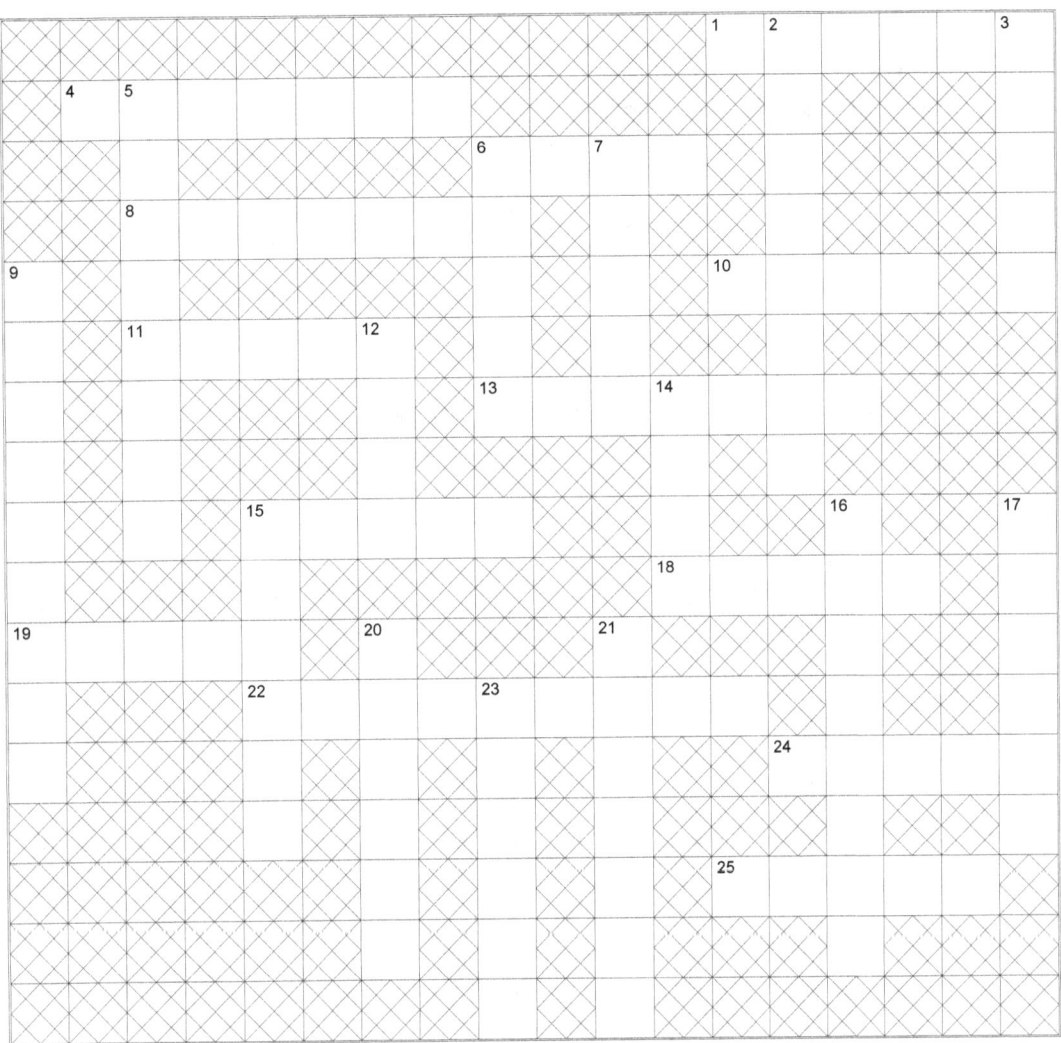

Across
1. According to Holden, these people were the biggest phonies of all
4. Lillian; DB's old girlfriend
6. Phoebe packed hers so she could go with Holden
8. Elevator operator who set Holden up with Sunny
10. Student at Whooton; had a drink with Holden
11. Holden's transportation to NY
13. History teacher
15. Allie's glove had these written on it
18. The prostitute
19. Holden calls people this when they do things that don't suit him
22. Narrator; Holden
24. Holden's dead brother
25. Holden lied to his mother on the train

Down
2. Holden watched Phoebe ride one
3. Holden's theater date
5. An ___ man wants to die nobly for a cause.
6. Little Shirley ___; record Holden bought Phoebe
7. Topic of the composition Holden wrote for Stradlater
9. Season to be jolly
12. Stradlater gave Holden a bloody one
14. Holden chatted with them at the sandwich bar
15. The school
16. English teacher
17. Roomed next to Holden at Pencey
20. Holden liked it because everything there stayed put
21. Holden returned to school with the ___ team
23. Holden was kicked out of Pencey because he ___

Catcher In The Rye Crossword 1 Answer Key

									1 A	2 C	T	O	R	3 S
	4 S	5 I	M	M	O	N	S			A				A
		M				6 B	7 A	G	S		R			L
	8 M	A	U	R	I	C	E		L		O			L
9 C		A				A			O	10 L	U	C	E	Y
H	11 T	R	A	I	12 N	N			V	S				
R	U				O	13 S	P	14 E	N	C	E	R		
I	R				S			U		L				
S	E	15 P	O	E	M	S		N		16 A			17 A	
T		E					18 S	U	N	N	Y		C	
19 M	O	R	O	N	20 M		21 F			T			K	
A		22 C	A	U	L	23 F	I	E	L	D			L	
S		E			S	A		N	24 A	L	L	I	E	
		Y			E	I		C	I				Y	
					U	L		I	25 E	R	N	I	E	
					M	E		N	I					
					D	G								

Across
1. According to Holden, these people were the biggest phonies of all
4. Lillian; DB's old girlfriend
6. Phoebe packed hers so she could go with Holden
8. Elevator operator who set Holden up with Sunny
10. Student at Whooton; had a drink with Holden
11. Holden's transportation to NY
13. History teacher
15. Allie's glove had these written on it
18. The prostitute
19. Holden calls people this when they do things that don't suit him
22. Narrator; Holden
24. Holden's dead brother
25. Holden lied to his mother on the train

Down
2. Holden watched Phoebe ride one
3. Holden's theater date
5. An ___ man wants to die nobly for a cause.
6. Little Shirley ___; record Holden bought Phoebe
7. Topic of the composition Holden wrote for Stradlater
9. Season to be jolly
12. Stradlater gave Holden a bloody one
14. Holden chatted with them at the sandwich bar
15. The school
16. English teacher
17. Roomed next to Holden at Pencey
20. Holden liked it because everything there stayed put
21. Holden returned to school with the ___ team
23. Holden was kicked out of Pencey because he ___

Catcher In The Rye Crossword 2

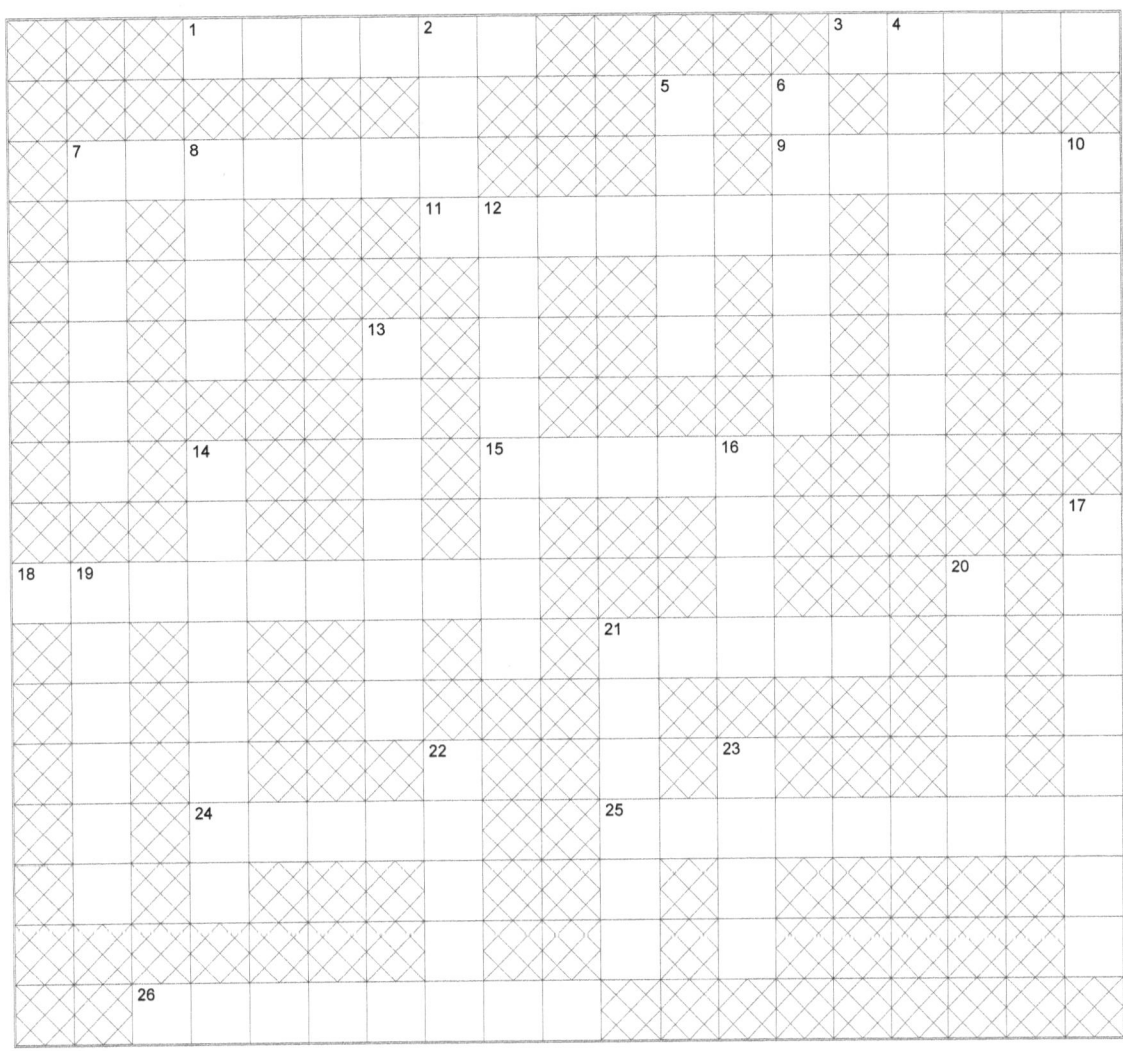

Across
1. Holden's sister
3. Holden's theater date
7. Holden returned to school with the ___ team
9. According to Holden, these people were the biggest phonies of all
11. Lillian; DB's old girlfriend
15. Holden's transportation to NY
18. Checker-playing neighbor friend of Holden: Jane ___
21. Allie's glove had these written on it
24. Holden lied to his mother on the train
25. Narrator; Holden
26. Holden watched Phoebe ride one

Down
2. Phoebe packed hers so she could go with Holden
4. English teacher
5. Topic of the composition Holden wrote for Stradlater
6. James ____ committed suicide
7. Holden was kicked out of Pencey because he ___
8. Holden chatted with them at the sandwich bar
10. The prostitute
12. An ___ man wants to die nobly for a cause.
13. The ___ In The Rye
14. Author
16. Stradlater gave Holden a bloody one
17. Bernice and friends danced with Holden at the ___ Room
19. Roomed next to Holden at Pencey
20. Holden's dead brother
21. The school
22. Little Shirley ___; record Holden bought Phoebe
23. Student at Whooton; had a drink with Holden

Catcher In The Rye Crossword 2 Answer Key

Across
1. Holden's sister
3. Holden's theater date
7. Holden returned to school with the ___ team
9. According to Holden, these people were the biggest phonies of all
11. Lillian; DB's old girlfriend
15. Holden's transportation to NY
18. Checker-playing neighbor friend of Holden: Jane ___
21. Allie's glove had these written on it
24. Holden lied to his mother on the train
25. Narrator; Holden
26. Holden watched Phoebe ride one

Down
2. Phoebe packed hers so she could go with Holden
4. English teacher
5. Topic of the composition Holden wrote for Stradlater
6. James ____ committed suicide
7. Holden was kicked out of Pencey because he ___
8. Holden chatted with them at the sandwich bar
10. The prostitute
12. An ___ man wants to die nobly for a cause.
13. The ___ In The Rye
14. Author
16. Stradlater gave Holden a bloody one
17. Bernice and friends danced with Holden at the ___ Room
19. Roomed next to Holden at Pencey
20. Holden's dead brother
21. The school
22. Little Shirley ___; record Holden bought Phoebe
23. Student at Whooton; had a drink with Holden

40
Copyrighted

Catcher In The Rye Crossword 3

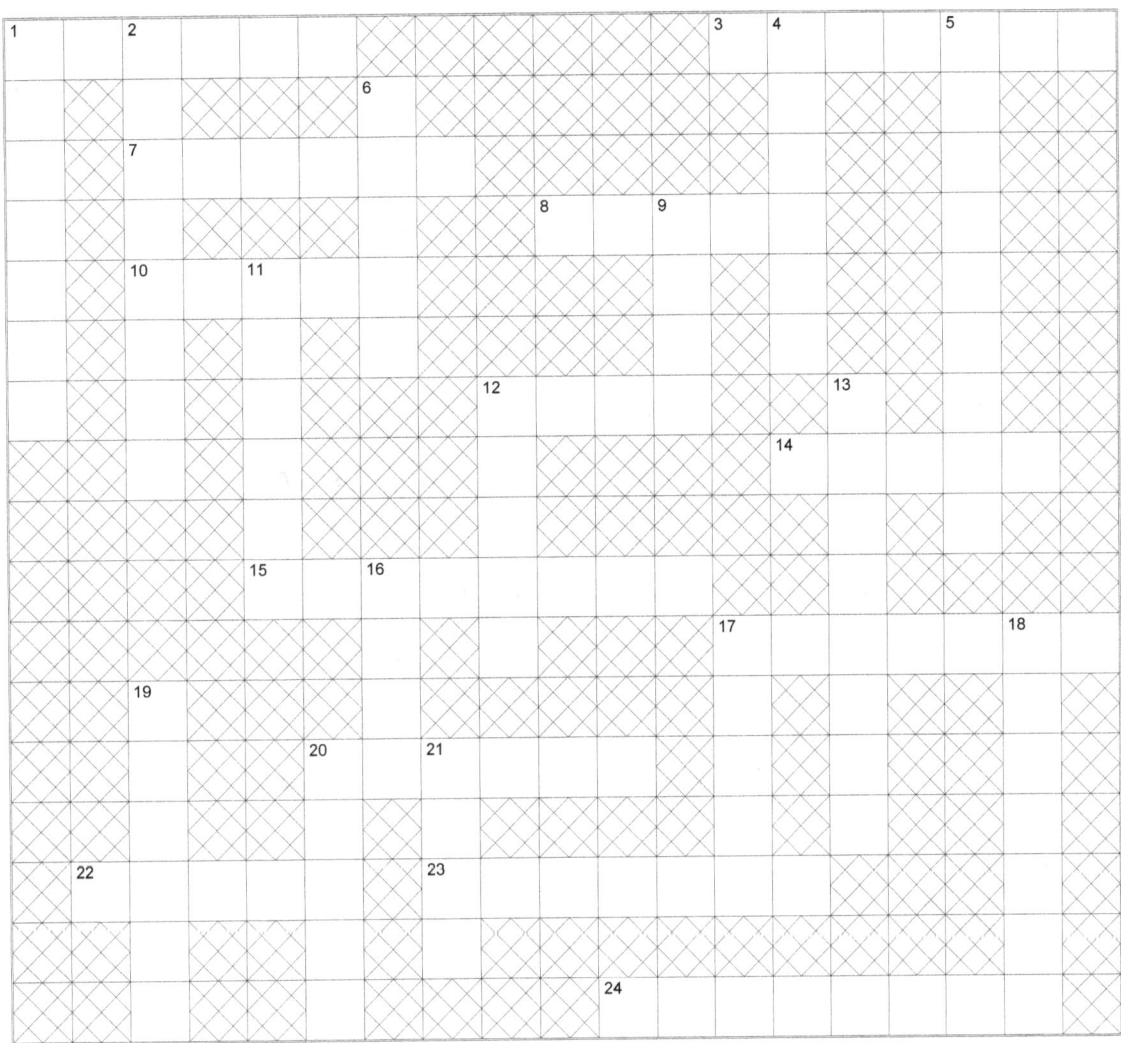

Across
1. Holden was kicked out of Pencey because he ___
3. History teacher
7. Holden liked it because everything there stayed put
8. Holden lied to his mother on the train
10. Holden's transportation to NY
12. Phoebe packed hers so she could go with Holden
14. Holden's theater date
15. Author
17. Elevator operator who set Holden up with Sunny
20. The school
22. Holden's dead brother
23. Lillian; DB's old girlfriend
24. Bernice and friends danced with Holden at the ___ Room

Down
1. Holden returned to school with the ___ team
2. An ___ man wants to die nobly for a cause.
4. Holden's sister
5. Narrator; Holden
6. The prostitute
9. Holden chatted with them at the sandwich bar
11. According to Holden, these people were the biggest phonies of all
12. Little Shirley ___; record Holden bought Phoebe
13. Holden watched Phoebe ride one
16. Student at Whooton; had a drink with Holden
17. Holden calls people this when they do things that don't suit him
18. The ___ In The Rye
19. Roomed next to Holden at Pencey
20. Allie's glove had these written on it
21. Stradlater gave Holden a bloody one

Catcher In The Rye Crossword 3 Answer Key

	1 F	2 A	I	L	E	D			3 S	4 P	E	N	5 C	E	R
	E		M			6 S				H			A		
	N	7 M	U	S	E	U	M			O			U		
	C		A			N		8 E	9 R	N	I	E		L	
	I	10 T	11 A	R	A	I	N		U		B		F		
	N		U		C		Y		N		E		I		
	G		R		T		12 B	A	G	S		13 C		E	
			E		O		E				14 S	A	L	L	Y
					R		A					R		D	
			15 S	16 A	L	I	N	G	E	R		O			
				U		S			17 M	A	U	R	I	18 C	E
		19 A		C					O		S			A	
		C			20 P	21 E	N	C	E	Y		R		E	
		K			O		O		R			E		T	
	22 A	L	L	I	E		23 S	I	M	M	O	N	S	C	H
		E			M		E							H	
		Y			S		24 L	A	V	E	N	D	E	R	

Across

1. Holden was kicked out of Pencey because he ___
3. History teacher
7. Holden liked it because everything there stayed put
8. Holden lied to his mother on the train
10. Holden's transportation to NY
12. Phoebe packed hers so she could go with Holden
14. Holden's theater date
15. Author
17. Elevator operator who set Holden up with Sunny
20. The school
22. Holden's dead brother
23. Lillian; DB's old girlfriend
24. Bernice and friends danced with Holden at the ___ Room

Down

1. Holden returned to school with the ___ team
2. An ___ man wants to die nobly for a cause.
4. Holden's sister
5. Narrator; Holden
6. The prostitute
9. Holden chatted with them at the sandwich bar
11. According to Holden, these people were the biggest phonies of all
12. Little Shirley ___; record Holden bought Phoebe
13. Holden watched Phoebe ride one
16. Student at Whooton; had a drink with Holden
17. Holden calls people this when they do things that don't suit him
18. The ___ In The Rye
19. Roomed next to Holden at Pencey
20. Allie's glove had these written on it
21. Stradlater gave Holden a bloody one

Catcher In The Rye Crossword 4

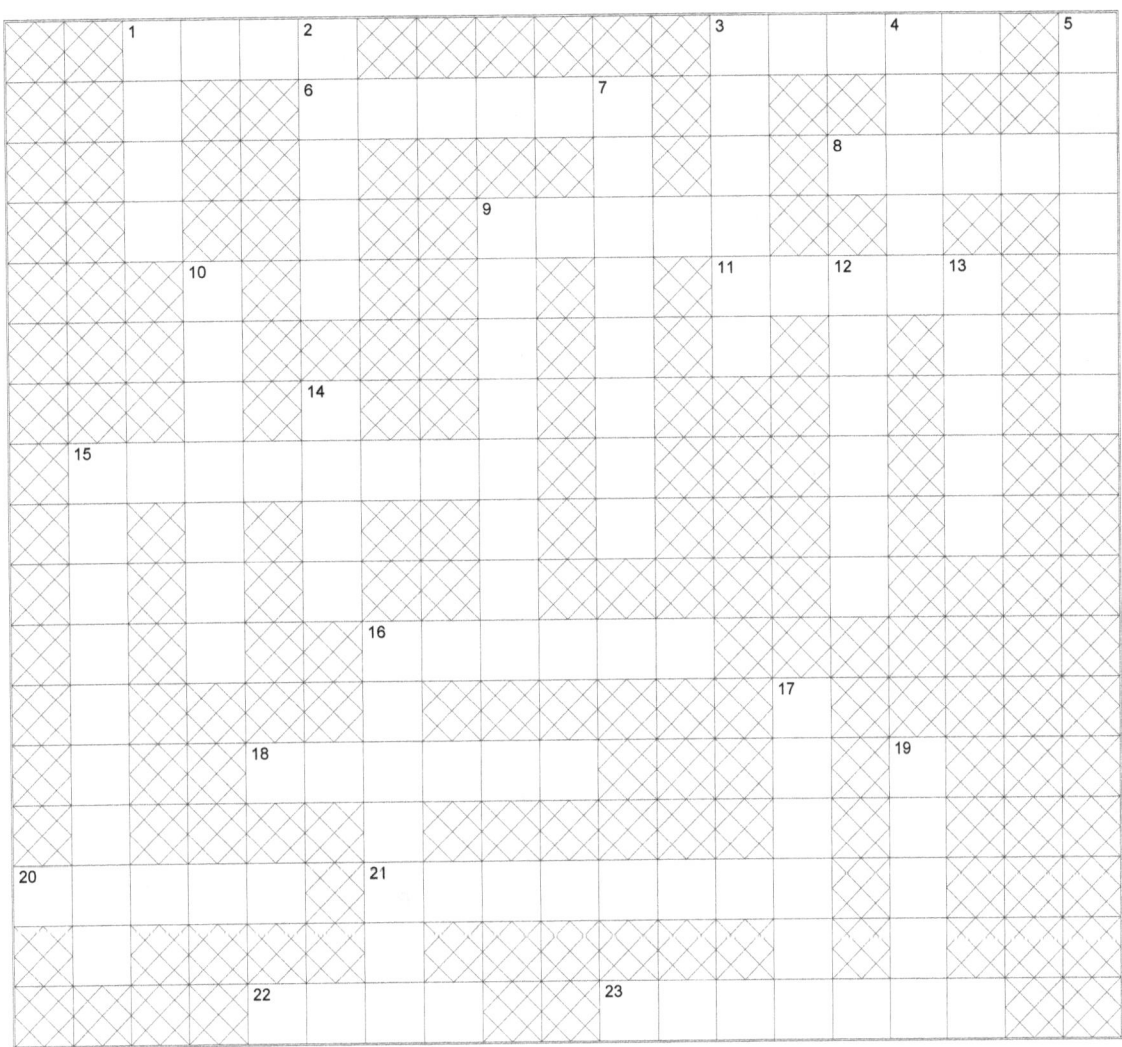

Across
1. Holden chatted with them at the sandwich bar
3. Allie's glove had these written on it
6. According to Holden, these people were the biggest phonies of all
8. Holden lied to his mother on the train
9. Holden's dead brother
11. Little Shirley ___; record Holden bought Phoebe
15. Holden watched Phoebe ride one
16. Holden was kicked out of Pencey because he ___
18. The school
20. Topic of the composition Holden wrote for Stradlater
21. An ___ man wants to die nobly for a cause.
22. Phoebe packed hers so she could go with Holden
23. Lillian; DB's old girlfriend

Down
1. Stradlater gave Holden a bloody one
2. Holden's theater date
3. Holden's sister
4. Holden calls people this when they do things that don't suit him
5. History teacher
7. Author
9. English teacher
10. Elevator operator who set Holden up with Sunny
12. Roomed next to Holden at Pencey
13. The prostitute
14. Student at Whooton; had a drink with Holden
15. Narrator; Holden
16. Holden returned to school with the ___ team
17. Holden liked it because everything there stayed put
19. Holden's transportation to NY

Catcher In The Rye Crossword 4 Answer Key

Across
1. Holden chatted with them at the sandwich bar
3. Allie's glove had these written on it
6. According to Holden, these people were the biggest phonies of all
8. Holden lied to his mother on the train
9. Holden's dead brother
11. Little Shirley ___; record Holden bought Phoebe
15. Holden watched Phoebe ride one
16. Holden was kicked out of Pencey because he ___
18. The school
20. Topic of the composition Holden wrote for Stradlater
21. An ___ man wants to die nobly for a cause.
22. Phoebe packed hers so she could go with Holden
23. Lillian; DB's old girlfriend

Down
1. Stradlater gave Holden a bloody one
2. Holden's theater date
3. Holden's sister
4. Holden calls people this when they do things that don't suit him
5. History teacher
7. Author
9. English teacher
10. Elevator operator who set Holden up with Sunny
12. Roomed next to Holden at Pencey
13. The prostitute
14. Student at Whooton; had a drink with Holden
15. Narrator; Holden
16. Holden returned to school with the ___ team
17. Holden liked it because everything there stayed put
19. Holden's transportation to NY

Catcher In The Rye

FENCING	MAURICE	IMMATURE	STRADLATER	ALLIE
NOSE	CAULFIELD	MUSEUM	PENCEY	TRAIN
SIMMONS	BAGS	FREE SPACE	NUNS	CHRISTMAS
LAVENDER	SALLY	ACTORS	ANTOLINI	MORON
SALINGER	FAILED	LUCE	CATCHER	GLOVE

Catcher In The Rye

SUNNY	SPENCER	GALLAGHER	POEMS	ACKLEY
PHOEBE	ERNIE	BEANS	CASTLE	GLOVE
CATCHER	LUCE	FREE SPACE	SALINGER	MORON
ANTOLINI	ACTORS	SALLY	LAVENDER	CHRISTMAS
NUNS	CAROUSEL	BAGS	SIMMONS	TRAIN

Catcher In The Rye

FENCING	STRADLATER	LAVENDER	SALLY	CAULFIELD
IMMATURE	ANTOLINI	PENCEY	TRAIN	ERNIE
GALLAGHER	SUNNY	FREE SPACE	BAGS	MORON
PHOEBE	MUSEUM	CATCHER	CAROUSEL	CASTLE
ACTORS	ACKLEY	MAURICE	SALINGER	LUCE

Catcher In The Rye

SPENCER	NOSE	CHRISTMAS	NUNS	GLOVE
ALLIE	BEANS	FAILED	SIMMONS	LUCE
SALINGER	MAURICE	FREE SPACE	ACTORS	CASTLE
CAROUSEL	CATCHER	MUSEUM	PHOEBE	MORON
BAGS	POEMS	SUNNY	GALLAGHER	ERNIE

Catcher In The Rye

CAULFIELD	SUNNY	MAURICE	CHRISTMAS	LUCE
ANTOLINI	CASTLE	NOSE	TRAIN	ALLIE
FENCING	SIMMONS	FREE SPACE	PENCEY	CATCHER
ACTORS	GALLAGHER	BAGS	FAILED	NUNS
ACKLEY	SALINGER	MUSEUM	BEANS	LAVENDER

Catcher In The Rye

SPENCER	CAROUSEL	MORON	ERNIE	GLOVE
SALLY	PHOEBE	POEMS	STRADLATER	LAVENDER
BEANS	MUSEUM	FREE SPACE	ACKLEY	NUNS
FAILED	BAGS	GALLAGHER	ACTORS	CATCHER
PENCEY	IMMATURE	SIMMONS	FENCING	ALLIE

Catcher In The Rye

POEMS	CASTLE	BAGS	FENCING	SALINGER
ACTORS	TRAIN	MUSEUM	GLOVE	BEANS
IMMATURE	STRADLATER	FREE SPACE	CAROUSEL	ERNIE
MORON	ACKLEY	SALLY	SUNNY	FAILED
NOSE	CAULFIELD	LUCE	ALLIE	SIMMONS

Catcher In The Rye

GALLAGHER	ANTOLINI	NUNS	SPENCER	MAURICE
LAVENDER	CATCHER	CHRISTMAS	PENCEY	SIMMONS
ALLIE	LUCE	FREE SPACE	NOSE	FAILED
SUNNY	SALLY	ACKLEY	MORON	ERNIE
CAROUSEL	PHOEBE	STRADLATER	IMMATURE	BEANS

Catcher In The Rye

LAVENDER	ACTORS	BAGS	ACKLEY	STRADLATER
CATCHER	SUNNY	NUNS	ALLIE	MAURICE
ANTOLINI	CHRISTMAS	FREE SPACE	TRAIN	NOSE
GALLAGHER	FAILED	POEMS	SPENCER	IMMATURE
CAROUSEL	SIMMONS	GLOVE	MORON	LUCE

Catcher In The Rye

CAULFIELD	PHOEBE	FENCING	CASTLE	SALLY
SALINGER	MUSEUM	BEANS	PENCEY	LUCE
MORON	GLOVE	FREE SPACE	CAROUSEL	IMMATURE
SPENCER	POEMS	FAILED	GALLAGHER	NOSE
TRAIN	ERNIE	CHRISTMAS	ANTOLINI	MAURICE

Catcher In The Rye

POEMS	SIMMONS	TRAIN	NOSE	SPENCER
GLOVE	MORON	BAGS	SALINGER	CAROUSEL
LAVENDER	CATCHER	FREE SPACE	SALLY	CHRISTMAS
PHOEBE	FAILED	PENCEY	ERNIE	MAURICE
GALLAGHER	NUNS	STRADLATER	ALLIE	CAULFIELD

Catcher In The Rye

MUSEUM	FENCING	CASTLE	ACKLEY	IMMATURE
BEANS	ANTOLINI	LUCE	ACTORS	CAULFIELD
ALLIE	STRADLATER	FREE SPACE	GALLAGHER	MAURICE
ERNIE	PENCEY	FAILED	PHOEBE	CHRISTMAS
SALLY	SUNNY	CATCHER	LAVENDER	CAROUSEL

Catcher In The Rye

IMMATURE	CASTLE	LUCE	LAVENDER	SALLY
FAILED	TRAIN	NUNS	SALINGER	POEMS
CHRISTMAS	SIMMONS	FREE SPACE	CAULFIELD	MUSEUM
ERNIE	PHOEBE	ANTOLINI	MORON	STRADLATER
ACTORS	SPENCER	PENCEY	ACKLEY	BAGS

Catcher In The Rye

ALLIE	GLOVE	SUNNY	CATCHER	GALLAGHER
BEANS	FENCING	MAURICE	NOSE	BAGS
ACKLEY	PENCEY	FREE SPACE	ACTORS	STRADLATER
MORON	ANTOLINI	PHOEBE	ERNIE	MUSEUM
CAULFIELD	CAROUSEL	SIMMONS	CHRISTMAS	POEMS

Catcher In The Rye

SALLY	CATCHER	FAILED	IMMATURE	ACTORS
CASTLE	PHOEBE	PENCEY	MORON	CAULFIELD
STRADLATER	SUNNY	FREE SPACE	GALLAGHER	BEANS
ANTOLINI	BAGS	SPENCER	CHRISTMAS	LAVENDER
ACKLEY	ERNIE	SALINGER	GLOVE	NOSE

Catcher In The Rye

CAROUSEL	LUCE	NUNS	TRAIN	POEMS
SIMMONS	MAURICE	FENCING	MUSEUM	NOSE
GLOVE	SALINGER	FREE SPACE	ACKLEY	LAVENDER
CHRISTMAS	SPENCER	BAGS	ANTOLINI	BEANS
GALLAGHER	ALLIE	SUNNY	STRADLATER	CAULFIELD

Catcher In The Rye

LUCE	SIMMONS	STRADLATER	SUNNY	GALLAGHER
SPENCER	CASTLE	FENCING	MAURICE	ACKLEY
PHOEBE	CAROUSEL	FREE SPACE	ACTORS	GLOVE
ANTOLINI	CHRISTMAS	IMMATURE	ALLIE	NOSE
BEANS	CAULFIELD	ERNIE	POEMS	SALLY

Catcher In The Rye

TRAIN	FAILED	MUSEUM	BAGS	SALINGER
MORON	LAVENDER	CATCHER	NUNS	SALLY
POEMS	ERNIE	FREE SPACE	BEANS	NOSE
ALLIE	IMMATURE	CHRISTMAS	ANTOLINI	GLOVE
ACTORS	PENCEY	CAROUSEL	PHOEBE	ACKLEY

Catcher In The Rye

PENCEY	IMMATURE	GLOVE	CAROUSEL	MORON
FAILED	CHRISTMAS	LUCE	SUNNY	CATCHER
BAGS	MAURICE	FREE SPACE	SPENCER	POEMS
TRAIN	NOSE	SALINGER	CAULFIELD	FENCING
MUSEUM	BEANS	SALLY	ALLIE	ERNIE

Catcher In The Rye

NUNS	SIMMONS	ANTOLINI	STRADLATER	ACKLEY
ACTORS	GALLAGHER	CASTLE	LAVENDER	ERNIE
ALLIE	SALLY	FREE SPACE	MUSEUM	FENCING
CAULFIELD	SALINGER	NOSE	TRAIN	POEMS
SPENCER	PHOEBE	MAURICE	BAGS	CATCHER

Catcher In The Rye

CATCHER	ACKLEY	NUNS	STRADLATER	IMMATURE
ANTOLINI	FENCING	ERNIE	PENCEY	MORON
LAVENDER	ALLIE	FREE SPACE	SPENCER	GLOVE
NOSE	POEMS	CHRISTMAS	PHOEBE	GALLAGHER
CAROUSEL	TRAIN	MUSEUM	ACTORS	FAILED

Catcher In The Rye

MAURICE	SIMMONS	SUNNY	CAULFIELD	SALINGER
CASTLE	LUCE	SALLY	BEANS	FAILED
ACTORS	MUSEUM	FREE SPACE	CAROUSEL	GALLAGHER
PHOEBE	CHRISTMAS	POEMS	NOSE	GLOVE
SPENCER	BAGS	ALLIE	LAVENDER	MORON

Catcher In The Rye

CATCHER	TRAIN	CAROUSEL	SALINGER	SUNNY
ANTOLINI	PENCEY	SPENCER	NOSE	ERNIE
BEANS	CASTLE	FREE SPACE	CHRISTMAS	SIMMONS
LAVENDER	LUCE	FAILED	PHOEBE	CAULFIELD
FENCING	MUSEUM	ACKLEY	STRADLATER	POEMS

Catcher In The Rye

GLOVE	NUNS	MAURICE	ACTORS	ALLIE
GALLAGHER	BAGS	IMMATURE	MORON	POEMS
STRADLATER	ACKLEY	FREE SPACE	FENCING	CAULFIELD
PHOEBE	FAILED	LUCE	LAVENDER	SIMMONS
CHRISTMAS	SALLY	CASTLE	BEANS	ERNIE

Catcher In The Rye

NOSE	CATCHER	LUCE	POEMS	BAGS
PHOEBE	ALLIE	SALLY	CAULFIELD	BEANS
TRAIN	ERNIE	FREE SPACE	IMMATURE	ACKLEY
STRADLATER	MAURICE	NUNS	SALINGER	LAVENDER
SUNNY	CHRISTMAS	CAROUSEL	MUSEUM	GLOVE

Catcher In The Rye

SIMMONS	FAILED	FENCING	PENCEY	SPENCER
GALLAGHER	ACTORS	ANTOLINI	CASTLE	GLOVE
MUSEUM	CAROUSEL	FREE SPACE	SUNNY	LAVENDER
SALINGER	NUNS	MAURICE	STRADLATER	ACKLEY
IMMATURE	MORON	ERNIE	TRAIN	BEANS

Catcher In The Rye

GALLAGHER	SALINGER	PHOEBE	POEMS	FAILED
LUCE	STRADLATER	ALLIE	CAULFIELD	MORON
BEANS	PENCEY	FREE SPACE	LAVENDER	ACTORS
TRAIN	CHRISTMAS	GLOVE	SPENCER	CATCHER
BAGS	ACKLEY	FENCING	CASTLE	IMMATURE

Catcher In The Rye

SIMMONS	CAROUSEL	NUNS	SUNNY	NOSE
SALLY	MUSEUM	MAURICE	ANTOLINI	IMMATURE
CASTLE	FENCING	FREE SPACE	BAGS	CATCHER
SPENCER	GLOVE	CHRISTMAS	TRAIN	ACTORS
LAVENDER	ERNIE	PENCEY	BEANS	MORON

Catcher In The Rye

ACKLEY	PHOEBE	STRADLATER	ANTOLINI	CAULFIELD
CASTLE	NUNS	POEMS	MORON	TRAIN
BEANS	SALINGER	FREE SPACE	LUCE	MAURICE
CAROUSEL	NOSE	ACTORS	SUNNY	CHRISTMAS
MUSEUM	BAGS	GALLAGHER	CATCHER	FAILED

Catcher In The Rye

SALLY	SIMMONS	FENCING	ERNIE	LAVENDER
IMMATURE	PENCEY	ALLIE	GLOVE	FAILED
CATCHER	GALLAGHER	FREE SPACE	MUSEUM	CHRISTMAS
SUNNY	ACTORS	NOSE	CAROUSEL	MAURICE
LUCE	SPENCER	SALINGER	BEANS	TRAIN

Catcher In The Rye

MUSEUM	LUCE	NUNS	POEMS	ANTOLINI
SALINGER	SALLY	NOSE	SPENCER	ACTORS
SUNNY	CAROUSEL	FREE SPACE	BAGS	BEANS
IMMATURE	MAURICE	ALLIE	CASTLE	LAVENDER
MORON	GLOVE	FENCING	ERNIE	GALLAGHER

Catcher In The Rye

FAILED	PENCEY	STRADLATER	SIMMONS	CHRISTMAS
CATCHER	CAULFIELD	ACKLEY	PHOEBE	GALLAGHER
ERNIE	FENCING	FREE SPACE	MORON	LAVENDER
CASTLE	ALLIE	MAURICE	IMMATURE	BEANS
BAGS	TRAIN	CAROUSEL	SUNNY	ACTORS

Catcher In The Rye Vocabulary Word List

No.	Word	Clue/Definition
1.	ARISTOCRATIC	Of an upper class; distinguished
2.	ATHEIST	A person who believes there is no God
3.	BLASE	Having done something so much as to be bored by it
4.	BOISTEROUS	Noisy; unruly
5.	BOURGEOIS	Smug; conventional; materialistic
6.	CAPACITY	Ability to contain, absorb, receive and hold
7.	COMPULSORY	Required; must be done
8.	CONSCIENTIOUS	Attentive to duty; diligent
9.	DIGRESSES	Rambles; departs temporarily from the main topic
10.	EXHIBITIONIST	One who likes to show off and get attention
11.	EXPEL	Drive out by force
12.	FASCINATED	Held the attention of; captivated
13.	FREQUENTLY	Often
14.	FROCK	Coat; cloak
15.	GROPING	Reaching blindly
16.	HALITOSIS	Bad smelling breath
17.	HEMORRHAGES	Bursting of blood vessels
18.	HUMBLE	Lowly; unpretentious
19.	INCOGNITO	In disguise
20.	INFERIORITY	Strong feelings of inadequacy
21.	INTIMATELY	Privately; personally; very closely
22.	IRONICAL	Meaning opposite of what is expressed
23.	LAVISH	Generous or liberal in giving or spending
24.	LOUSE	A person regarded as mean or contemptible
25.	NONCHALANT	Showing a lack of concern; casually indifferent
26.	OSTRACIZED	Shunned; excluded; left out
27.	PACIFIST	One who opposed the use of force under any circumstances
28.	PEDAGOGICAL	Characteristic of teaching or teachers
29.	PUTRID	Rotten
30.	QUALMS	Feelings of doubt
31.	RANDOM	Haphazardly; without careful choice; by chance
32.	RASPY	Grating
33.	RECIPROCAL	Mutual; equivalent; interchangeable
34.	SADISTIC	Getting pleasure from inflicting pain on others
35.	SOPHISTICATED	Worldly wise; refined
36.	STENOGRAPHER	A person skilled in taking shorthand
37.	SWANKY	Expensive and showy
38.	UNANIMOUS	Showing or based on total agreement
39.	UNSCRUPULOUS	Having no moral code; unprincipled

Copyrighted

Catcher In The Rye Vocabulary Fill In The Blank 1

_____ 1. A person skilled in taking shorthand

_____ 2. One who likes to show off and get attention

_____ 3. Rotten

_____ 4. A person who believes there is no God

_____ 5. Required; must be done

_____ 6. One who opposed the use of force under any circumstances

_____ 7. Rambles; departs temporarily from the main topic

_____ 8. Bad smelling breath

_____ 9. Bursting of blood vessels

_____ 10. Lowly; unpretentious

_____ 11. Having done something so much as to be bored by it

_____ 12. Worldly wise; refined

_____ 13. Ability to contain, absorb, receive and hold

_____ 14. Mutual; equivalent; interchangeable

_____ 15. Showing or based on total agreement

_____ 16. Feelings of doubt

_____ 17. Noisy; unruly

_____ 18. In disguise

_____ 19. Coat; cloak

_____ 20. Meaning opposite of what is expressed

Catcher In The Rye Vocabulary Fill In The Blank 1 Answer Key

STENOGRAPHER	1. A person skilled in taking shorthand
EXHIBITIONIST	2. One who likes to show off and get attention
PUTRID	3. Rotten
ATHEIST	4. A person who believes there is no God
COMPULSORY	5. Required; must be done
PACIFIST	6. One who opposed the use of force under any circumstances
DIGRESSES	7. Rambles; departs temporarily from the main topic
HALITOSIS	8. Bad smelling breath
HEMORRHAGES	9. Bursting of blood vessels
HUMBLE	10. Lowly; unpretentious
BLASE	11. Having done something so much as to be bored by it
SOPHISTICATED	12. Worldly wise; refined
CAPACITY	13. Ability to contain, absorb, receive and hold
RECIPROCAL	14. Mutual; equivalent; interchangeable
UNANIMOUS	15. Showing or based on total agreement
QUALMS	16. Feelings of doubt
BOISTEROUS	17. Noisy; unruly
INCOGNITO	18. In disguise
FROCK	19. Coat; cloak
IRONICAL	20. Meaning opposite of what is expressed

Catcher In The Rye Vocabulary Fill In The Blank 2

_____ 1. Lowly; unpretentious

_____ 2. Ability to contain, absorb, receive and hold

_____ 3. Drive out by force

_____ 4. Required; must be done

_____ 5. Noisy; unruly

_____ 6. Characteristic of teaching or teachers

_____ 7. Shunned; excluded; left out

_____ 8. Having done something so much as to be bored by it

_____ 9. Showing a lack of concern; casually indifferent

_____ 10. Generous or liberal in giving or spending

_____ 11. Rotten

_____ 12. Coat; cloak

_____ 13. Having no moral code; unprincipled

_____ 14. A person who believes there is no God

_____ 15. Meaning opposite of what is expressed

_____ 16. A person skilled in taking shorthand

_____ 17. Getting pleasure from inflicting pain on others

_____ 18. Strong feelings of inadequacy

_____ 19. Mutual; equivalent; interchangeable

_____ 20. One who likes to show off and get attention

Catcher In The Rye Vocabulary Fill In The Blank 2 Answer Key

HUMBLE	1. Lowly; unpretentious
CAPACITY	2. Ability to contain, absorb, receive and hold
EXPEL	3. Drive out by force
COMPULSORY	4. Required; must be done
BOISTEROUS	5. Noisy; unruly
PEDAGOGICAL	6. Characteristic of teaching or teachers
OSTRACIZED	7. Shunned; excluded; left out
BLASE	8. Having done something so much as to be bored by it
NONCHALANT	9. Showing a lack of concern; casually indifferent
LAVISH	10. Generous or liberal in giving or spending
PUTRID	11. Rotten
FROCK	12. Coat; cloak
UNSCRUPULOUS	13. Having no moral code; unprincipled
ATHEIST	14. A person who believes there is no God
IRONICAL	15. Meaning opposite of what is expressed
STENOGRAPHER	16. A person skilled in taking shorthand
SADISTIC	17. Getting pleasure from inflicting pain on others
INFERIORITY	18. Strong feelings of inadequacy
RECIPROCAL	19. Mutual; equivalent; interchangeable
EXHIBITIONIST	20. One who likes to show off and get attention

Catcher In The Rye Vocabulary Fill In The Blank 3

_____ 1. Of an upper class; distinguished

_____ 2. Showing or based on total agreement

_____ 3. Having no moral code; unprincipled

_____ 4. Bursting of blood vessels

_____ 5. Worldly wise; refined

_____ 6. Rambles; departs temporarily from the main topic

_____ 7. Required; must be done

_____ 8. Lowly; unpretentious

_____ 9. Reaching blindly

_____ 10. Privately; personally; very closely

_____ 11. Getting pleasure from inflicting pain on others

_____ 12. Strong feelings of inadequacy

_____ 13. Expensive and showy

_____ 14. One who likes to show off and get attention

_____ 15. Noisy; unruly

_____ 16. Characteristic of teaching or teachers

_____ 17. Rotten

_____ 18. Meaning opposite of what is expressed

_____ 19. Ability to contain, absorb, receive and hold

_____ 20. Coat; cloak

Catcher In The Rye Vocabulary Fill In The Blank 3 Answer Key

ARISTOCRATIC	1. Of an upper class; distinguished
UNANIMOUS	2. Showing or based on total agreement
UNSCRUPULOUS	3. Having no moral code; unprincipled
HEMORRHAGES	4. Bursting of blood vessels
SOPHISTICATED	5. Worldly wise; refined
DIGRESSES	6. Rambles; departs temporarily from the main topic
COMPULSORY	7. Required; must be done
HUMBLE	8. Lowly; unpretentious
GROPING	9. Reaching blindly
INTIMATELY	10. Privately; personally; very closely
SADISTIC	11. Getting pleasure from inflicting pain on others
INFERIORITY	12. Strong feelings of inadequacy
SWANKY	13. Expensive and showy
EXHIBITIONIST	14. One who likes to show off and get attention
BOISTEROUS	15. Noisy; unruly
PEDAGOGICAL	16. Characteristic of teaching or teachers
PUTRID	17. Rotten
IRONICAL	18. Meaning opposite of what is expressed
CAPACITY	19. Ability to contain, absorb, receive and hold
FROCK	20. Coat; cloak

Catcher In The Rye Vocabulary Fill In The Blank 4

_____ 1. One who opposed the use of force under any circumstances
_____ 2. A person regarded as mean or contemptible
_____ 3. Worldly wise; refined
_____ 4. Haphazardly; without careful choice; by chance
_____ 5. Mutual; equivalent; interchangeable
_____ 6. Rotten
_____ 7. Drive out by force
_____ 8. A person who believes there is no God
_____ 9. Ability to contain, absorb, receive and hold
_____ 10. Showing or based on total agreement
_____ 11. Generous or liberal in giving or spending
_____ 12. Getting pleasure from inflicting pain on others
_____ 13. Reaching blindly
_____ 14. Smug; conventional; materialistic
_____ 15. Bursting of blood vessels
_____ 16. Rambles; departs temporarily from the main topic
_____ 17. Showing a lack of concern; casually indifferent
_____ 18. Shunned; excluded; left out
_____ 19. Required; must be done
_____ 20. Coat; cloak

Catcher In The Rye Vocabulary Fill In The Blank 4 Answer Key

PACIFIST	1. One who opposed the use of force under any circumstances
LOUSE	2. A person regarded as mean or contemptible
SOPHISTICATED	3. Worldly wise; refined
RANDOM	4. Haphazardly; without careful choice; by chance
RECIPROCAL	5. Mutual; equivalent; interchangeable
PUTRID	6. Rotten
EXPEL	7. Drive out by force
ATHEIST	8. A person who believes there is no God
CAPACITY	9. Ability to contain, absorb, receive and hold
UNANIMOUS	10. Showing or based on total agreement
LAVISH	11. Generous or liberal in giving or spending
SADISTIC	12. Getting pleasure from inflicting pain on others
GROPING	13. Reaching blindly
BOURGEOIS	14. Smug; conventional; materialistic
HEMORRHAGES	15. Bursting of blood vessels
DIGRESSES	16. Rambles; departs temporarily from the main topic
NONCHALANT	17. Showing a lack of concern; casually indifferent
OSTRACIZED	18. Shunned; excluded; left out
COMPULSORY	19. Required; must be done
FROCK	20. Coat; cloak

Catcher In The Rye Vocabulary Matching 1

___ 1. ATHEIST A. Reaching blindly
___ 2. FASCINATED B. Bursting of blood vessels
___ 3. IRONICAL C. Held the attention of; captivated
___ 4. FREQUENTLY D. Rambles; departs temporarily from the main topic
___ 5. HALITOSIS E. Noisy; unruly
___ 6. INFERIORITY F. One who likes to show off and get attention
___ 7. RANDOM G. Lowly; unpretentious
___ 8. SOPHISTICATED H. Bad smelling breath
___ 9. RECIPROCAL I. A person skilled in taking shorthand
___ 10. BOISTEROUS J. Haphazardly; without careful choice; by chance
___ 11. UNSCRUPULOUS K. Attentive to duty; diligent
___ 12. CAPACITY L. Smug; conventional; materialistic
___ 13. INCOGNITO M. Characteristic of teaching or teachers
___ 14. CONSCIENTIOUS N. In disguise
___ 15. DIGRESSES O. Having no moral code; unprincipled
___ 16. UNANIMOUS P. Often
___ 17. GROPING Q. Mutual; equivalent; interchangeable
___ 18. NONCHALANT R. Drive out by force
___ 19. EXHIBITIONIST S. Ability to contain, absorb, receive and hold
___ 20. HUMBLE T. Strong feelings of inadequacy
___ 21. PEDAGOGICAL U. Meaning opposite of what is expressed
___ 22. HEMORRHAGES V. A person who believes there is no God
___ 23. BOURGEOIS W. Showing or based on total agreement
___ 24. EXPEL X. Worldly wise; refined
___ 25. STENOGRAPHER Y. Showing a lack of concern; casually indifferent

Catcher In The Rye Vocabulary Matching 1 Answer Key

V - 1. ATHEIST	A.	Reaching blindly
C - 2. FASCINATED	B.	Bursting of blood vessels
U - 3. IRONICAL	C.	Held the attention of; captivated
P - 4. FREQUENTLY	D.	Rambles; departs temporarily from the main topic
H - 5. HALITOSIS	E.	Noisy; unruly
T - 6. INFERIORITY	F.	One who likes to show off and get attention
J - 7. RANDOM	G.	Lowly; unpretentious
X - 8. SOPHISTICATED	H.	Bad smelling breath
Q - 9. RECIPROCAL	I.	A person skilled in taking shorthand
E -10. BOISTEROUS	J.	Haphazardly; without careful choice; by chance
O -11. UNSCRUPULOUS	K.	Attentive to duty; diligent
S -12. CAPACITY	L.	Smug; conventional; materialistic
N -13. INCOGNITO	M.	Characteristic of teaching or teachers
K -14. CONSCIENTIOUS	N.	In disguise
D -15. DIGRESSES	O.	Having no moral code; unprincipled
W -16. UNANIMOUS	P.	Often
A -17. GROPING	Q.	Mutual; equivalent; interchangeable
Y -18. NONCHALANT	R.	Drive out by force
F -19. EXHIBITIONIST	S.	Ability to contain, absorb, receive and hold
G -20. HUMBLE	T.	Strong feelings of inadequacy
M -21. PEDAGOGICAL	U.	Meaning opposite of what is expressed
B -22. HEMORRHAGES	V.	A person who believes there is no God
L -23. BOURGEOIS	W.	Showing or based on total agreement
R -24. EXPEL	X.	Worldly wise; refined
I -25. STENOGRAPHER	Y.	Showing a lack of concern; casually indifferent

Catcher In The Rye Vocabulary Matching 2

___ 1. RASPY
___ 2. FASCINATED
___ 3. RANDOM
___ 4. LOUSE
___ 5. LAVISH
___ 6. EXHIBITIONIST
___ 7. QUALMS
___ 8. SWANKY
___ 9. CAPACITY
___ 10. HEMORRHAGES
___ 11. INTIMATELY
___ 12. HUMBLE
___ 13. COMPULSORY
___ 14. BOISTEROUS
___ 15. INFERIORITY
___ 16. NONCHALANT
___ 17. PUTRID
___ 18. UNSCRUPULOUS
___ 19. UNANIMOUS
___ 20. IRONICAL
___ 21. FREQUENTLY
___ 22. OSTRACIZED
___ 23. HALITOSIS
___ 24. GROPING
___ 25. FROCK

A. One who likes to show off and get attention
B. Noisy; unruly
C. Bad smelling breath
D. Showing or based on total agreement
E. Having no moral code; unprincipled
F. Shunned; excluded; left out
G. Rotten
H. Feelings of doubt
I. Required; must be done
J. Often
K. A person regarded as mean or contemptible
L. Reaching blindly
M. Meaning opposite of what is expressed
N. Strong feelings of inadequacy
O. Grating
P. Expensive and showy
Q. Privately; personally; very closely
R. Lowly; unpretentious
S. Generous or liberal in giving or spending
T. Ability to contain, absorb, receive and hold
U. Haphazardly; without careful choice; by chance
V. Coat; cloak
W. Showing a lack of concern; casually indifferent
X. Held the attention of; captivated
Y. Bursting of blood vessels

Catcher In The Rye Vocabulary Matching 2 Answer Key

O - 1. RASPY
X - 2. FASCINATED
U - 3. RANDOM
K - 4. LOUSE
S - 5. LAVISH
A - 6. EXHIBITIONIST
H - 7. QUALMS
P - 8. SWANKY
T - 9. CAPACITY
Y - 10. HEMORRHAGES
Q - 11. INTIMATELY
R - 12. HUMBLE
I - 13. COMPULSORY
B - 14. BOISTEROUS
N - 15. INFERIORITY
W - 16. NONCHALANT
G - 17. PUTRID
E - 18. UNSCRUPULOUS
D - 19. UNANIMOUS
M - 20. IRONICAL
J - 21. FREQUENTLY
F - 22. OSTRACIZED
C - 23. HALITOSIS
L - 24. GROPING
V - 25. FROCK

A. One who likes to show off and get attention
B. Noisy; unruly
C. Bad smelling breath
D. Showing or based on total agreement
E. Having no moral code; unprincipled
F. Shunned; excluded; left out
G. Rotten
H. Feelings of doubt
I. Required; must be done
J. Often
K. A person regarded as mean or contemptible
L. Reaching blindly
M. Meaning opposite of what is expressed
N. Strong feelings of inadequacy
O. Grating
P. Expensive and showy
Q. Privately; personally; very closely
R. Lowly; unpretentious
S. Generous or liberal in giving or spending
T. Ability to contain, absorb, receive and hold
U. Haphazardly; without careful choice; by chance
V. Coat; cloak
W. Showing a lack of concern; casually indifferent
X. Held the attention of; captivated
Y. Bursting of blood vessels

Catcher In The Rye Vocabulary Matching 3

___ 1. HALITOSIS   A. Ability to contain, absorb, receive and hold
___ 2. RANDOM   B. Bad smelling breath
___ 3. PACIFIST   C. One who likes to show off and get attention
___ 4. LAVISH   D. Held the attention of; captivated
___ 5. ATHEIST   E. In disguise
___ 6. SOPHISTICATED   F. Generous or liberal in giving or spending
___ 7. UNSCRUPULOUS   G. Coat; cloak
___ 8. IRONICAL   H. Expensive and showy
___ 9. COMPULSORY   I. Meaning opposite of what is expressed
___10. EXHIBITIONIST   J. Privately; personally; very closely
___11. FROCK   K. Rotten
___12. RECIPROCAL   L. Of an upper class; distinguished
___13. SADISTIC   M. One who opposed the use of force under any circumstances
___14. INTIMATELY   N. Haphazardly; without careful choice; by chance
___15. PUTRID   O. Having done something so much as to be bored by it
___16. ARISTOCRATIC   P. Mutual; equivalent; interchangeable
___17. FREQUENTLY   Q. A person who believes there is no God
___18. FASCINATED   R. Attentive to duty; diligent
___19. CAPACITY   S. Noisy; unruly
___20. HEMORRHAGES   T. Having no moral code; unprincipled
___21. BOISTEROUS   U. Bursting of blood vessels
___22. INCOGNITO   V. Getting pleasure from inflicting pain on others
___23. BLASE   W. Often
___24. SWANKY   X. Worldly wise; refined
___25. CONSCIENTIOUS   Y. Required; must be done

Catcher In The Rye Vocabulary Matching 3 Answer Key

- B - 1. HALITOSIS
- N - 2. RANDOM
- M - 3. PACIFIST
- F - 4. LAVISH
- Q - 5. ATHEIST
- X - 6. SOPHISTICATED
- T - 7. UNSCRUPULOUS
- I - 8. IRONICAL
- Y - 9. COMPULSORY
- C - 10. EXHIBITIONIST
- G - 11. FROCK
- P - 12. RECIPROCAL
- V - 13. SADISTIC
- J - 14. INTIMATELY
- K - 15. PUTRID
- L - 16. ARISTOCRATIC
- W - 17. FREQUENTLY
- D - 18. FASCINATED
- A - 19. CAPACITY
- U - 20. HEMORRHAGES
- S - 21. BOISTEROUS
- E - 22. INCOGNITO
- O - 23. BLASE
- H - 24. SWANKY
- R - 25. CONSCIENTIOUS

A. Ability to contain, absorb, receive and hold
B. Bad smelling breath
C. One who likes to show off and get attention
D. Held the attention of; captivated
E. In disguise
F. Generous or liberal in giving or spending
G. Coat; cloak
H. Expensive and showy
I. Meaning opposite of what is expressed
J. Privately; personally; very closely
K. Rotten
L. Of an upper class; distinguished
M. One who opposed the use of force under any circumstances
N. Haphazardly; without careful choice; by chance
O. Having done something so much as to be bored by it
P. Mutual; equivalent; interchangeable
Q. A person who believes there is no God
R. Attentive to duty; diligent
S. Noisy; unruly
T. Having no moral code; unprincipled
U. Bursting of blood vessels
V. Getting pleasure from inflicting pain on others
W. Often
X. Worldly wise; refined
Y. Required; must be done

Catcher In The Rye Vocabulary Matching 4

___ 1. UNSCRUPULOUS   A. Showing or based on total agreement
___ 2. NONCHALANT   B. Mutual; equivalent; interchangeable
___ 3. SWANKY   C. Of an upper class; distinguished
___ 4. SADISTIC   D. Drive out by force
___ 5. CONSCIENTIOUS   E. Characteristic of teaching or teachers
___ 6. FROCK   F. Feelings of doubt
___ 7. INTIMATELY   G. Having done something so much as to be bored by it
___ 8. EXHIBITIONIST   H. Shunned; excluded; left out
___ 9. ARISTOCRATIC   I. Expensive and showy
___ 10. PACIFIST   J. Bad smelling breath
___ 11. DIGRESSES   K. Reaching blindly
___ 12. LOUSE   L. Showing a lack of concern; casually indifferent
___ 13. PEDAGOGICAL   M. Haphazardly; without careful choice; by chance
___ 14. BLASE   N. Rambles; departs temporarily from the main topic
___ 15. RECIPROCAL   O. A person regarded as mean or contemptible
___ 16. CAPACITY   P. Smug; conventional; materialistic
___ 17. GROPING   Q. Worldly wise; refined
___ 18. HALITOSIS   R. One who likes to show off and get attention
___ 19. EXPEL   S. Privately; personally; very closely
___ 20. UNANIMOUS   T. Getting pleasure from inflicting pain on others
___ 21. RANDOM   U. Coat; cloak
___ 22. OSTRACIZED   V. Ability to contain, absorb, receive and hold
___ 23. QUALMS   W. Having no moral code; unprincipled
___ 24. SOPHISTICATED   X. Attentive to duty; diligent
___ 25. BOURGEOIS   Y. One who opposed the use of force under any circumstances

Catcher In The Rye Vocabulary Matching 4 Answer Key

W - 1. UNSCRUPULOUS
L - 2. NONCHALANT
I - 3. SWANKY
T - 4. SADISTIC
X - 5. CONSCIENTIOUS
U - 6. FROCK
S - 7. INTIMATELY
R - 8. EXHIBITIONIST
C - 9. ARISTOCRATIC
Y - 10. PACIFIST
N - 11. DIGRESSES
O - 12. LOUSE
E - 13. PEDAGOGICAL
G - 14. BLASE
B - 15. RECIPROCAL
V - 16. CAPACITY
K - 17. GROPING
J - 18. HALITOSIS
D - 19. EXPEL
A - 20. UNANIMOUS
M - 21. RANDOM
H - 22. OSTRACIZED
F - 23. QUALMS
Q - 24. SOPHISTICATED
P - 25. BOURGEOIS

A. Showing or based on total agreement
B. Mutual; equivalent; interchangeable
C. Of an upper class; distinguished
D. Drive out by force
E. Characteristic of teaching or teachers
F. Feelings of doubt
G. Having done something so much as to be bored by it
H. Shunned; excluded; left out
I. Expensive and showy
J. Bad smelling breath
K. Reaching blindly
L. Showing a lack of concern; casually indifferent
M. Haphazardly; without careful choice; by chance
N. Rambles; departs temporarily from the main topic
O. A person regarded as mean or contemptible
P. Smug; conventional; materialistic
Q. Worldly wise; refined
R. One who likes to show off and get attention
S. Privately; personally; very closely
T. Getting pleasure from inflicting pain on others
U. Coat; cloak
V. Ability to contain, absorb, receive and hold
W. Having no moral code; unprincipled
X. Attentive to duty; diligent
Y. One who opposed the use of force under any circumstances

Catcher In The Rye Vocabulary Magic Squares 1

Match the definition with the vocabulary word. Put your answers in the magic squares below. When your answers are correct, all columns and rows will add to the same number.

A. BOURGEOIS
B. RECIPROCAL
C. CAPACITY
D. SOPHISTICATED
E. RASPY
F. UNANIMOUS
G. PEDAGOGICAL
H. PUTRID
I. GROPING
J. HUMBLE
K. RANDOM
L. EXPEL
M. DIGRESSES
N. HEMORRHAGES
O. INFERIORITY
P. PACIFIST

1. Smug; conventional; materialistic
2. Bursting of blood vessels
3. Lowly; unpretentious
4. Grating
5. Characteristic of teaching or teachers
6. Drive out by force
7. One who opposed the use of force under any circumstances
8. Ability to contain, absorb, receive and hold
9. Strong feelings of inadequacy
10. Worldly wise; refined
11. Rotten
12. Haphazardly; without careful choice; by chance
13. Reaching blindly
14. Showing or based on total agreement
15. Mutual; equivalent; interchangeable
16. Rambles; departs temporarily from the main topic

A=	B=	C=	D=
E=	F=	G=	H=
I=	J=	K=	L=
M=	N=	O=	P=

Catcher In The Rye Vocabulary Magic Squares 1 Answer Key

Match the definition with the vocabulary word. Put your answers in the magic squares below. When your answers are correct, all columns and rows will add to the same number.

A. BOURGEOIS
B. RECIPROCAL
C. CAPACITY
D. SOPHISTICATED
E. RASPY
F. UNANIMOUS
G. PEDAGOGICAL
H. PUTRID
I. GROPING
J. HUMBLE
K. RANDOM
L. EXPEL
M. DIGRESSES
N. HEMORRHAGES
O. INFERIORITY
P. PACIFIST

1. Smug; conventional; materialistic
2. Bursting of blood vessels
3. Lowly; unpretentious
4. Grating
5. Characteristic of teaching or teachers
6. Drive out by force
7. One who opposed the use of force under any circumstances
8. Ability to contain, absorb, receive and hold
9. Strong feelings of inadequacy
10. Worldly wise; refined
11. Rotten
12. Haphazardly; without careful choice; by chance
13. Reaching blindly
14. Showing or based on total agreement
15. Mutual; equivalent; interchangeable
16. Rambles; departs temporarily from the main topic

A=1	B=15	C=8	D=10
E=4	F=14	G=5	H=11
I=13	J=3	K=12	L=6
M=16	N=2	O=9	P=7

Catcher In The Rye Vocabulary Magic Squares 2

Match the definition with the vocabulary word. Put your answers in the magic squares below. When your answers are correct, all columns and rows will add to the same number.

A. RECIPROCAL
B. STENOGRAPHER
C. INTIMATELY
D. SOPHISTICATED
E. PUTRID
F. RASPY
G. FREQUENTLY
H. FROCK
I. COMPULSORY
J. UNSCRUPULOUS
K. HUMBLE
L. UNANIMOUS
M. IRONICAL
N. DIGRESSES
O. BOISTEROUS
P. HALITOSIS

1. A person skilled in taking shorthand
2. Often
3. Lowly; unpretentious
4. Rambles; departs temporarily from the main topic
5. Meaning opposite of what is expressed
6. Showing or based on total agreement
7. Coat; cloak
8. Mutual; equivalent; interchangeable
9. Bad smelling breath
10. Required; must be done
11. Rotten
12. Worldly wise; refined
13. Privately; personally; very closely
14. Grating
15. Having no moral code; unprincipled
16. Noisy; unruly

A=	B=	C=	D=
E=	F=	G=	H=
I=	J=	K=	L=
M=	N=	O=	P=

Catcher In The Rye Vocabulary Magic Squares 2 Answer Key

Match the definition with the vocabulary word. Put your answers in the magic squares below. When your answers are correct, all columns and rows will add to the same number.

A. RECIPROCAL
B. STENOGRAPHER
C. INTIMATELY
D. SOPHISTICATED
E. PUTRID
F. RASPY
G. FREQUENTLY
H. FROCK
I. COMPULSORY
J. UNSCRUPULOUS
K. HUMBLE
L. UNANIMOUS
M. IRONICAL
N. DIGRESSES
O. BOISTEROUS
P. HALITOSIS

1. A person skilled in taking shorthand
2. Often
3. Lowly; unpretentious
4. Rambles; departs temporarily from the main topic
5. Meaning opposite of what is expressed
6. Showing or based on total agreement
7. Coat; cloak
8. Mutual; equivalent; interchangeable
9. Bad smelling breath
10. Required; must be done
11. Rotten
12. Worldly wise; refined
13. Privately; personally; very closely
14. Grating
15. Having no moral code; unprincipled
16. Noisy; unruly

A=8	B=1	C=13	D=12
E=11	F=14	G=2	H=7
I=10	J=15	K=3	L=6
M=5	N=4	O=16	P=9

Copyrighted

Catcher In The Rye Vocabulary Magic Squares 3

Match the definition with the vocabulary word. Put your answers in the magic squares below. When your answers are correct, all columns and rows will add to the same number.

A. FREQUENTLY
B. SOPHISTICATED
C. INTIMATELY
D. PEDAGOGICAL
E. LOUSE
F. HALITOSIS
G. INCOGNITO
H. PACIFIST
I. EXPEL
J. SADISTIC
K. ATHEIST
L. QUALMS
M. BOISTEROUS
N. STENOGRAPHER
O. BOURGEOIS
P. ARISTOCRATIC

1. Smug; conventional; materialistic
2. Getting pleasure from inflicting pain on others
3. One who opposed the use of force under any circumstances
4. Often
5. Characteristic of teaching or teachers
6. A person regarded as mean or contemptible
7. A person who believes there is no God
8. A person skilled in taking shorthand
9. Bad smelling breath
10. Privately; personally; very closely
11. Noisy; unruly
12. Feelings of doubt
13. Drive out by force
14. Of an upper class; distinguished
15. Worldly wise; refined
16. In disguise

A=	B=	C=	D=
E=	F=	G=	H=
I=	J=	K=	L=
M=	N=	O=	P=

Catcher In The Rye Vocabulary Magic Squares 3 Answer Key

Match the definition with the vocabulary word. Put your answers in the magic squares below. When your answers are correct, all columns and rows will add to the same number.

A. FREQUENTLY
B. SOPHISTICATED
C. INTIMATELY
D. PEDAGOGICAL
E. LOUSE
F. HALITOSIS
G. INCOGNITO
H. PACIFIST
I. EXPEL
J. SADISTIC
K. ATHEIST
L. QUALMS
M. BOISTEROUS
N. STENOGRAPHER
O. BOURGEOIS
P. ARISTOCRATIC

1. Smug; conventional; materialistic
2. Getting pleasure from inflicting pain on others
3. One who opposed the use of force under any circumstances
4. Often
5. Characteristic of teaching or teachers
6. A person regarded as mean or contemptible
7. A person who believes there is no God
8. A person skilled in taking shorthand
9. Bad smelling breath
10. Privately; personally; very closely
11. Noisy; unruly
12. Feelings of doubt
13. Drive out by force
14. Of an upper class; distinguished
15. Worldly wise; refined
16. In disguise

A=4	B=15	C=10	D=5
E=6	F=9	G=16	H=3
I=13	J=2	K=7	L=12
M=11	N=8	O=1	P=14

Catcher In The Rye Vocabulary Magic Squares 4

Match the definition with the vocabulary word. Put your answers in the magic squares below. When your answers are correct, all columns and rows will add to the same number.

A. ATHEIST
B. CAPACITY
C. SOPHISTICATED
D. ARISTOCRATIC
E. HUMBLE
F. QUALMS
G. BLASE
H. FROCK
I. DIGRESSES
J. UNSCRUPULOUS
K. SADISTIC
L. BOURGEOIS
M. INCOGNITO
N. INTIMATELY
O. PUTRID
P. SWANKY

1. Ability to contain, absorb, receive and hold
2. Having done something so much as to be bored by it
3. Getting pleasure from inflicting pain on others
4. Privately; personally; very closely
5. In disguise
6. Smug; conventional; materialistic
7. Coat; cloak
8. A person who believes there is no God
9. Expensive and showy
10. Rambles; departs temporarily from the main topic
11. Lowly; unpretentious
12. Of an upper class; distinguished
13. Worldly wise; refined
14. Feelings of doubt
15. Having no moral code; unprincipled
16. Rotten

A=	B=	C=	D=
E=	F=	G=	H=
I=	J=	K=	L=
M=	N=	O=	P=

Catcher In The Rye Vocabulary Magic Squares 4 Answer Key

Match the definition with the vocabulary word. Put your answers in the magic squares below. When your answers are correct, all columns and rows will add to the same number.

A. ATHEIST
B. CAPACITY
C. SOPHISTICATED
D. ARISTOCRATIC
E. HUMBLE
F. QUALMS
G. BLASE
H. FROCK
I. DIGRESSES
J. UNSCRUPULOUS
K. SADISTIC
L. BOURGEOIS
M. INCOGNITO
N. INTIMATELY
O. PUTRID
P. SWANKY

1. Ability to contain, absorb, receive and hold
2. Having done something so much as to be bored by it
3. Getting pleasure from inflicting pain on others
4. Privately; personally; very closely
5. In disguise
6. Smug; conventional; materialistic
7. Coat; cloak
8. A person who believes there is no God
9. Expensive and showy
10. Rambles; departs temporarily from the main topic
11. Lowly; unpretentious
12. Of an upper class; distinguished
13. Worldly wise; refined
14. Feelings of doubt
15. Having no moral code; unprincipled
16. Rotten

A=8	B=1	C=13	D=12
E=11	F=14	G=2	H=7
I=10	J=15	K=3	L=6
M=5	N=4	O=16	P=9

Catcher In The Rye Vocabulary Word Search 1

Words are placed backwards, forward, diagonally, up and down. Clues listed below can help you find the words. Circle the hidden vocabulary words in the maze.

```
D D Q B W T D B Y H H H T W B C H Q R G
E P J O G C E L J N S C S B G I A B A N
T U D U O S T R A C I Z E D Q T L C N M
A T M R B S A E Y I V C R W S A I O D P
N R V G I N C H N T A M M I S R T M O V
I I D E F O I P S S L V F E E C O P M G
C D H O R N T A G I R I H T X O S U B K
S T F I E C S R X D C A S Q P T I L O D
A U R S Q H I G J A G I S T E S S S I J
F N O F U A H O P S N H J P L I E O S Z
X A C M E L P N L O U S E Y Y R G R T W
L N K N N A O E I Q M H L T B A A Y E Z
W I M B T N S T I L V E B I N G H H R B
B M W S L T I S A R T Y M C S R R N O C
B O K X Y B W U K A O K U A Z O R S U W
Q U J S I R Q B M X M N H P S P O X S V
C S V H N B F I D G T A I A K I M K T H
Y X X G Y X T G N R Z W M C X N E Q K C
C E O T I N G O C N I S N X A G H G J G
X X Y T I R O I R E F N I R P L V N F K
```

A person regarded as mean or contemptible (5)
A person skilled in taking shorthand (12)
A person who believes there is no God (7)
Ability to contain, absorb, receive and hold (8)
Bad smelling breath (9)
Bursting of blood vessels (11)
Coat; cloak (5)
Drive out by force (5)
Expensive and showy (6)
Feelings of doubt (6)
Generous or liberal in giving or spending (6)
Getting pleasure from inflicting pain on others (8)
Grating (5)
Haphazardly; without careful choice; by chance (6)
Having done something so much as to be bored by it (5)
Held the attention of; captivated (10)

In disguise (9)
Lowly; unpretentious (6)
Meaning opposite of what is expressed (8)
Noisy; unruly (10)
Of an upper class; distinguished (12)
Often (10)
One who likes to show off and get attention (13)
One who opposed the use of force under any circumstances (8)
Privately; personally; very closely (10)
Reaching blindly (7)
Required; must be done (10)
Rotten (6)
Showing a lack of concern; casually indifferent (10)
Showing or based on total agreement (9)
Shunned; excluded; left out (10)
Smug; conventional; materialistic (9)
Strong feelings of inadequacy (11)
Worldly wise; refined (13)

Catcher In The Rye Vocabulary Word Search 1 Answer Key

Words are placed backwards, forward, diagonally, up and down. Clues listed below can help you find the words. Circle the hidden vocabulary words in the maze.

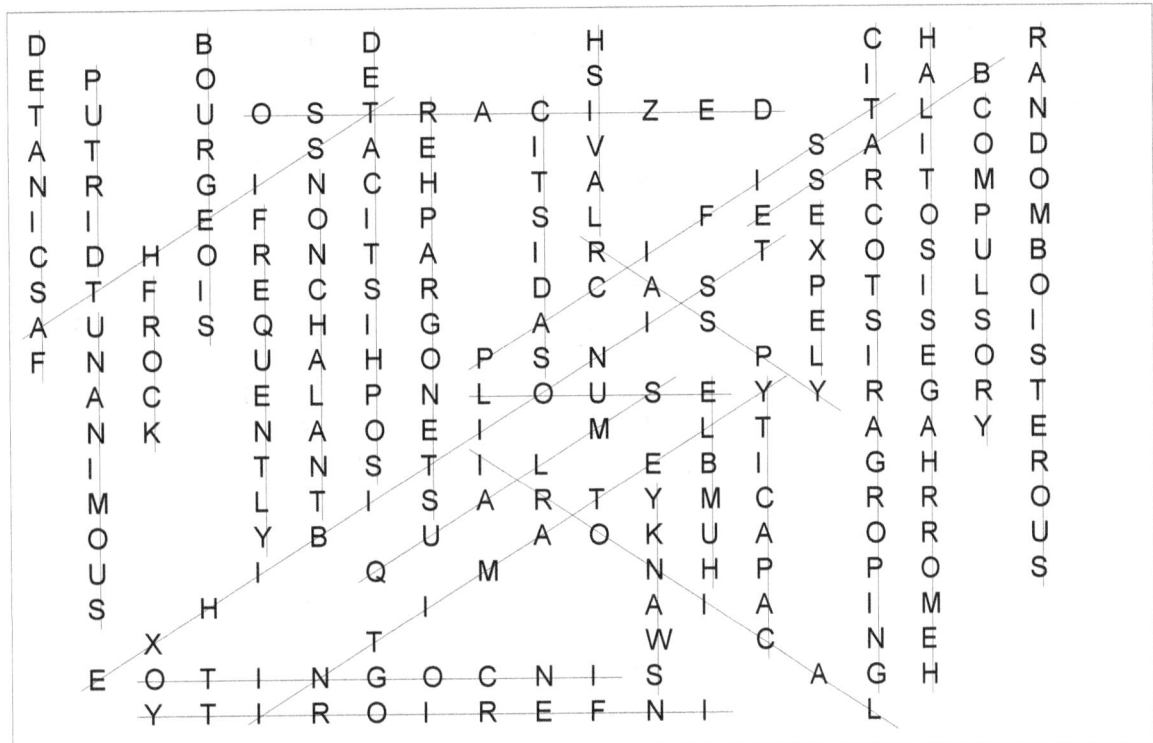

A person regarded as mean or contemptible (5)
A person skilled in taking shorthand (12)
A person who believes there is no God (7)
Ability to contain, absorb, receive and hold (8)
Bad smelling breath (9)
Bursting of blood vessels (11)
Coat; cloak (5)
Drive out by force (5)
Expensive and showy (6)
Feelings of doubt (6)
Generous or liberal in giving or spending (6)
Getting pleasure from inflicting pain on others (8)
Grating (5)
Haphazardly; without careful choice; by chance (6)
Having done something so much as to be bored by it (5)
Held the attention of; captivated (10)

In disguise (9)
Lowly; unpretentious (6)
Meaning opposite of what is expressed (8)
Noisy; unruly (10)
Of an upper class; distinguished (12)
Often (10)
One who likes to show off and get attention (13)
One who opposed the use of force under any circumstances (8)
Privately; personally; very closely (10)
Reaching blindly (7)
Required; must be done (10)
Rotten (6)
Showing a lack of concern; casually indifferent (10)
Showing or based on total agreement (9)
Shunned; excluded; left out (10)
Smug; conventional; materialistic (9)
Strong feelings of inadequacy (11)
Worldly wise; refined (13)

Catcher In The Rye Vocabulary Word Search 2

Words are placed backwards, forward, diagonally, up and down. Clues listed below can help you find the words. Circle the hidden vocabulary words in the maze.

```
H B H S U O I T N E I C S N O C J R S X
E A N A B O I S T E R O U S O Z C O F W
M W L D E Z I C A R T S O T L M P T R B
O Y T I R O I R E F N I I S A H J S E B
R H R S T J Y Z P Y N C R I L L I Q D
R V G T S O Z Q M D G N I S C D Z E U M
H S P I I Z S Y G O D S T P M H W H E T
A T H C F V J I C R T I Z V Z S F T N J
G E L D I H G N S O C U G W N V G A T D
E N A E C Y I C C A Q N L R V Y L R L T
S O C T A L R R T W Z A Q V E A S Z Y B
F G I A P E A E A N K N S M H S G W L D
Q R N N T T D X Q N N I G C Z T S R O W
R A O I I A R Z Z W D M N G V L X E U H
T P R C S M L A U Q B O U R G E O I S B
Z H I S K I E G S L N U M O R C F I E J
W E P A D T P Y A P X S V P B K V P W B
K R G F L N X S X K Y Y T I C A P A C F
C F F G C I E G Q Q Q T C N L W L T G N
H U M B L E P U T R I D C G S W A N K Y
```

A person regarded as mean or contemptible (5)
A person skilled in taking shorthand (12)
A person who believes there is no God (7)
Ability to contain, absorb, receive and hold (8)
Attentive to duty; diligent (13)
Bad smelling breath (9)
Bursting of blood vessels (11)
Coat; cloak (5)
Drive out by force (5)
Expensive and showy (6)
Feelings of doubt (6)
Generous or liberal in giving or spending (6)
Getting pleasure from inflicting pain on others (8)
Grating (5)
Haphazardly; without careful choice; by chance (6)
Having done something so much as to be bored by it (5)

Held the attention of; captivated (10)
In disguise (9)
Lowly; unpretentious (6)
Meaning opposite of what is expressed (8)
Noisy; unruly (10)
Of an upper class; distinguished (12)
Often (10)
One who opposed the use of force under any circumstances (8)
Privately; personally; very closely (10)
Rambles; departs temporarily from the main topic (9)
Reaching blindly (7)
Rotten (6)
Showing a lack of concern; casually indifferent (10)
Showing or based on total agreement (9)
Shunned; excluded; left out (10)
Smug; conventional; materialistic (9)
Strong feelings of inadequacy (11)
Worldly wise; refined (13)

Catcher In The Rye Vocabulary Word Search 2 Answer Key

Words are placed backwards, forward, diagonally, up and down. Clues listed below can help you find the words. Circle the hidden vocabulary words in the maze.

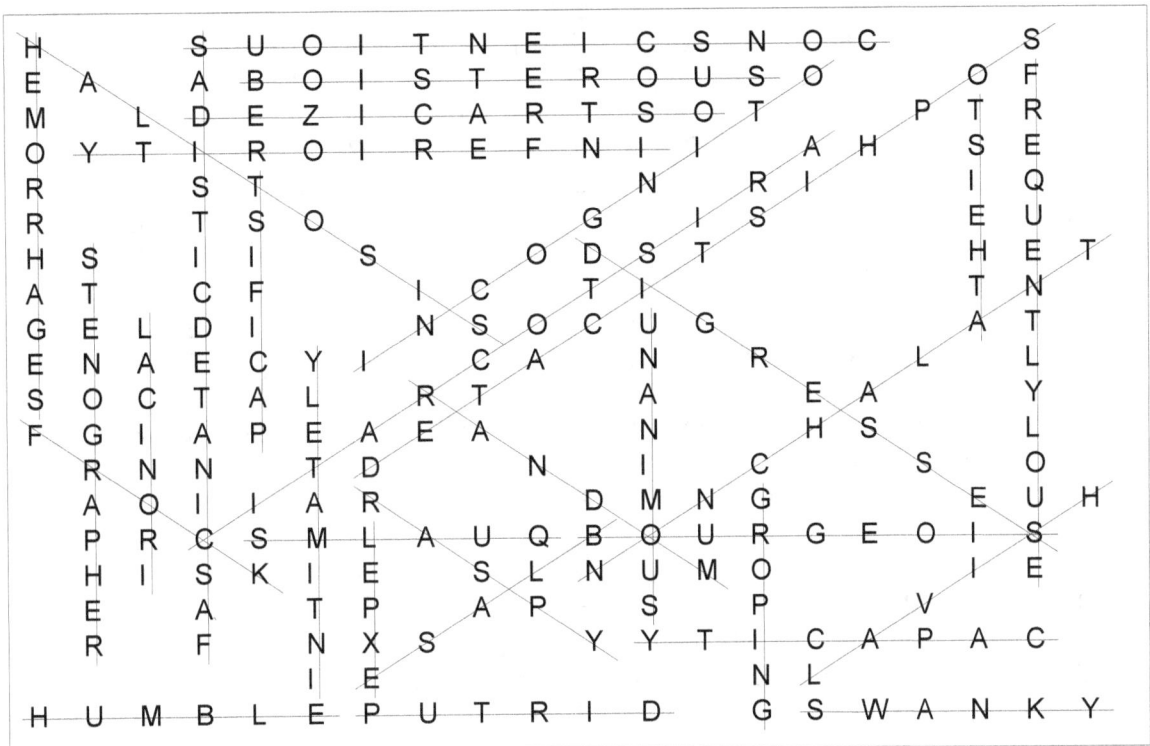

A person regarded as mean or contemptible (5)
A person skilled in taking shorthand (12)
A person who believes there is no God (7)
Ability to contain, absorb, receive and hold (8)
Attentive to duty; diligent (13)
Bad smelling breath (9)
Bursting of blood vessels (11)
Coat; cloak (5)
Drive out by force (5)
Expensive and showy (6)
Feelings of doubt (6)
Generous or liberal in giving or spending (6)
Getting pleasure from inflicting pain on others (8)
Grating (5)
Haphazardly; without careful choice; by chance (6)
Having done something so much as to be bored by it (5)

Held the attention of; captivated (10)
In disguise (9)
Lowly; unpretentious (6)
Meaning opposite of what is expressed (8)
Noisy; unruly (10)
Of an upper class; distinguished (12)
Often (10)
One who opposed the use of force under any circumstances (8)
Privately; personally; very closely (10)
Rambles; departs temporarily from the main topic (9)
Reaching blindly (7)
Rotten (6)
Showing a lack of concern; casually indifferent (10)
Showing or based on total agreement (9)
Shunned; excluded; left out (10)
Smug; conventional; materialistic (9)
Strong feelings of inadequacy (11)
Worldly wise; refined (13)

Catcher In The Rye Vocabulary Word Search 3

Words are placed backwards, forward, diagonally, up and down. Words listed below are included in the maze. Circle the hidden vocabulary words in the maze.

```
G N O N C H A L A N T H F C D H H B O M
R E H P A R G O N E T S I O I U X O S K
O M M B P R S L P R I J N G M X U T R Z
P B F D A P Y O S Q R S C S R B T R A C
I P A R C C R P P Z O R O C E L Y G A C
N W S H I D O H C H N R G I S E J E C H
G X C B T G S X I Q I A N E S Q F O I P
H V I N Y A L L T H C S I N E T S I Z G
J L N Z L T U P A B A P T T S C U S E D
Y N A V K H P K R S L Y O I J D O P D G
L R T V W E M R C S C O N O C Y R W I F
T X E N I I O C O Y B O U U H A E N K N
N W D W Q S C I T S I D A S P U T R I D
E Z H Y J T H W S T F D W T E I S E G W
U V R F H X N F I F Q A N X M F I G D X
Q U A L M S X B R C N E L A X J O H D W
E J N R M J I O A K S E T N S F B S P K
R F D D H H C W Y A P E M V C B M B R Y
F Z O Q X K D F L X L P A C I F I S T H
H S M E P V D B E Y R E C I P R O C A L
```

ARISTOCRATIC

ATHEIST

BLASE

BOISTEROUS

BOURGEOIS

CAPACITY

COMPULSORY

CONSCIENTIOUS

DIGRESSES

EXHIBITIONIST

EXPEL

FASCINATED

FREQUENTLY

FROCK

GROPING

HUMBLE

INCOGNITO

INTIMATELY

IRONICAL

LAVISH

LOUSE

NONCHALANT

OSTRACIZED

PACIFIST

PUTRID

QUALMS

RANDOM

RASPY

RECIPROCAL

SADISTIC

SOPHISTICATED

STENOGRAPHER

SWANKY

Catcher In The Rye Vocabulary Word Search 3 Answer Key

Words are placed backwards, forward, diagonally, up and down. Words listed below are included in the maze. Circle the hidden vocabulary words in the maze.

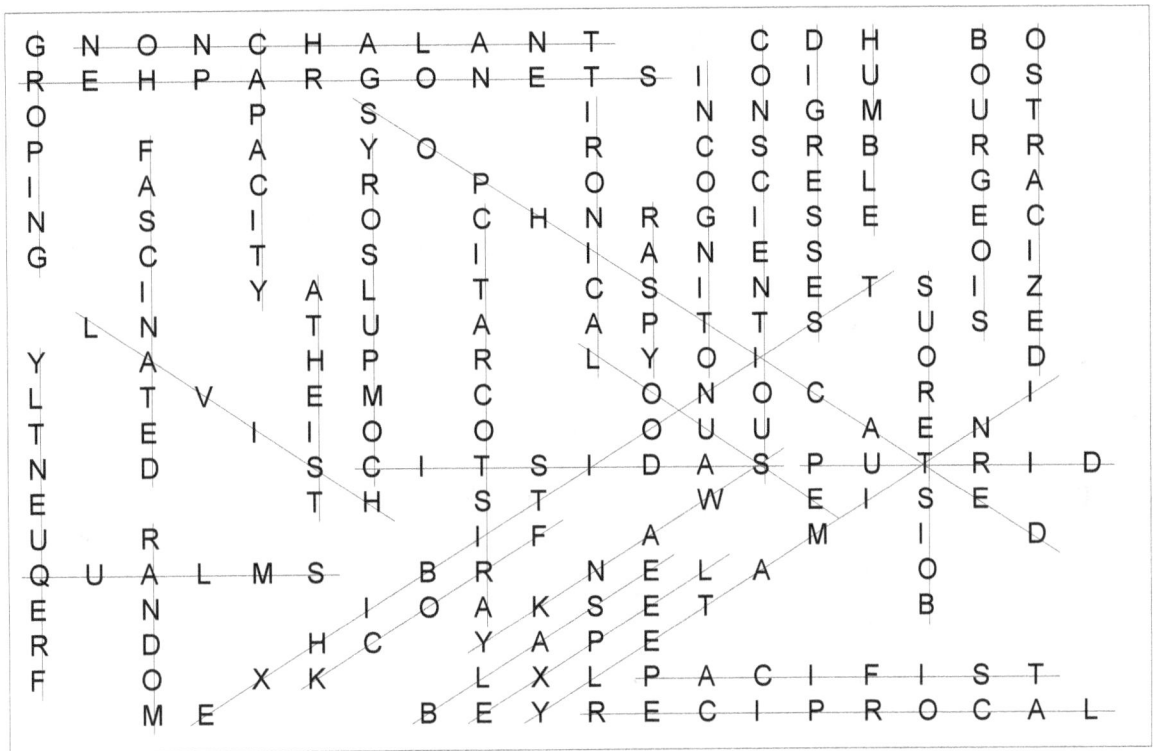

ARISTOCRATIC	FASCINATED	OSTRACIZED
ATHEIST	FREQUENTLY	PACIFIST
BLASE	FROCK	PUTRID
BOISTEROUS	GROPING	QUALMS
BOURGEOIS	HUMBLE	RANDOM
CAPACITY	INCOGNITO	RASPY
COMPULSORY	INTIMATELY	RECIPROCAL
CONSCIENTIOUS	IRONICAL	SADISTIC
DIGRESSES	LAVISH	SOPHISTICATED
EXHIBITIONIST	LOUSE	STENOGRAPHER
EXPEL	NONCHALANT	SWANKY

Catcher In The Rye Vocabulary Word Search 4

Words are placed backwards, forward, diagonally, up and down. Words listed below are included in the maze. Circle the hidden vocabulary words in the maze.

```
S C A P A C I T Y N O N C H A L A N T H
W D H R A M N C O M P U L S O R Y F H M
A Z U E I C T F A S C I N A T E D T A N
N T M C N F I R O N I C A L D M G G L Z
K G B I F W M F X J C L S X E S J M I F
Y D L P E D A C I Q C S R L Z M N N T L
V C E R R I T G L S J M P O I R M B O V
F V R O I G E R B X T L H U C R O B S V
Y P S C O R L X N D M A S S A U R V I J
P U X A R E Y L T N E U Q E R F C Y S M
E T F L I S J L W L O Q X G T X R A N V
D R U H T S H X P L Q P E H S X D O T Q
A I P N Y E H F U Y E O Z T O I S T C C
G D B L A S E P Y L I N R A S P Y I G K
O H C K I N U X Q S V K T T R H H N R W
G L L V M R I D Q H D H I H Z D H G O P
I C A C C B K M S C Z C Z E M G K O P Z
C L C S T S I N O I T I B I H X E C I Y
A V N T L V Q R D U D C J S D Q J N S P
L U R A N D O M H H S Y V T S T S I G P
```

ATHEIST	GROPING	PACIFIST
BLASE	HALITOSIS	PEDAGOGICAL
BOURGEOIS	HUMBLE	PUTRID
CAPACITY	INCOGNITO	QUALMS
COMPULSORY	INFERIORITY	RANDOM
DIGRESSES	INTIMATELY	RASPY
EXHIBITIONIST	IRONICAL	RECIPROCAL
EXPEL	LAVISH	SADISTIC
FASCINATED	LOUSE	SWANKY
FREQUENTLY	NONCHALANT	UNANIMOUS
FROCK	OSTRACIZED	UNSCRUPULOUS

Catcher In The Rye Vocabulary Word Search 4 Answer Key

Words are placed backwards, forward, diagonally, up and down. Words listed below are included in the maze. Circle the hidden vocabulary words in the maze.

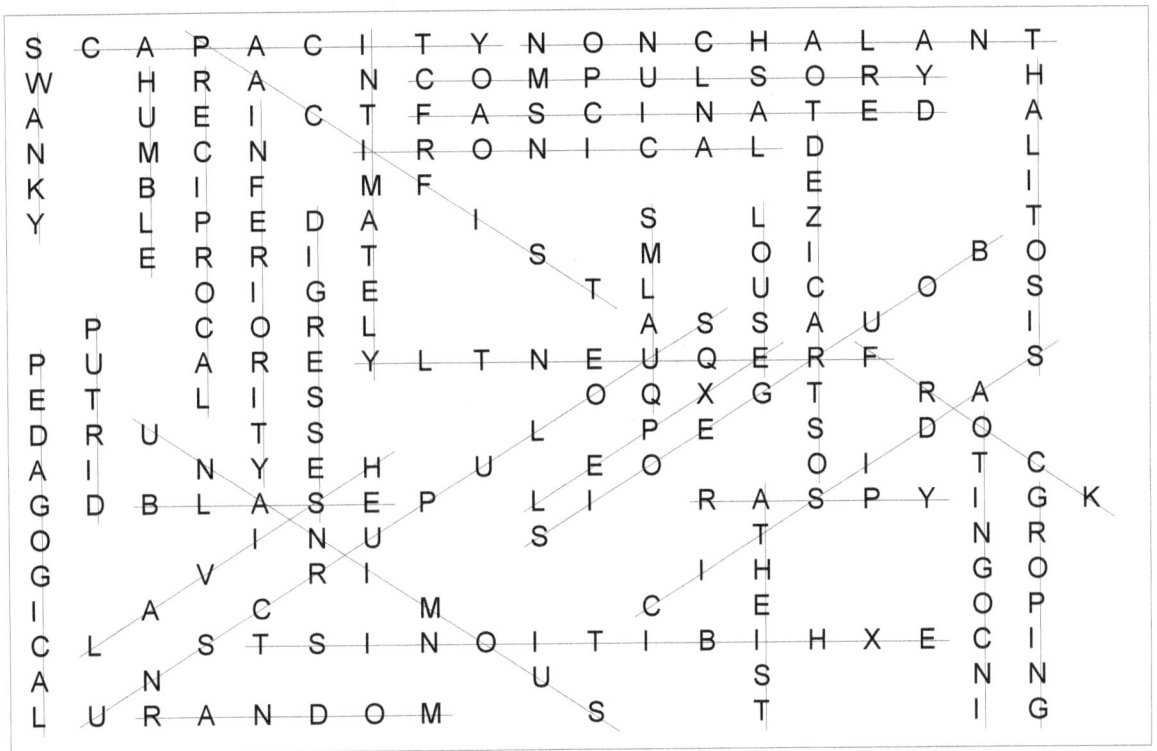

ATHEIST	GROPING	PACIFIST
BLASE	HALITOSIS	PEDAGOGICAL
BOURGEOIS	HUMBLE	PUTRID
CAPACITY	INCOGNITO	QUALMS
COMPULSORY	INFERIORITY	RANDOM
DIGRESSES	INTIMATELY	RASPY
EXHIBITIONIST	IRONICAL	RECIPROCAL
EXPEL	LAVISH	SADISTIC
FASCINATED	LOUSE	SWANKY
FREQUENTLY	NONCHALANT	UNANIMOUS
FROCK	OSTRACIZED	UNSCRUPULOUS

Catcher In The Rye Vocabulary Crossword 1

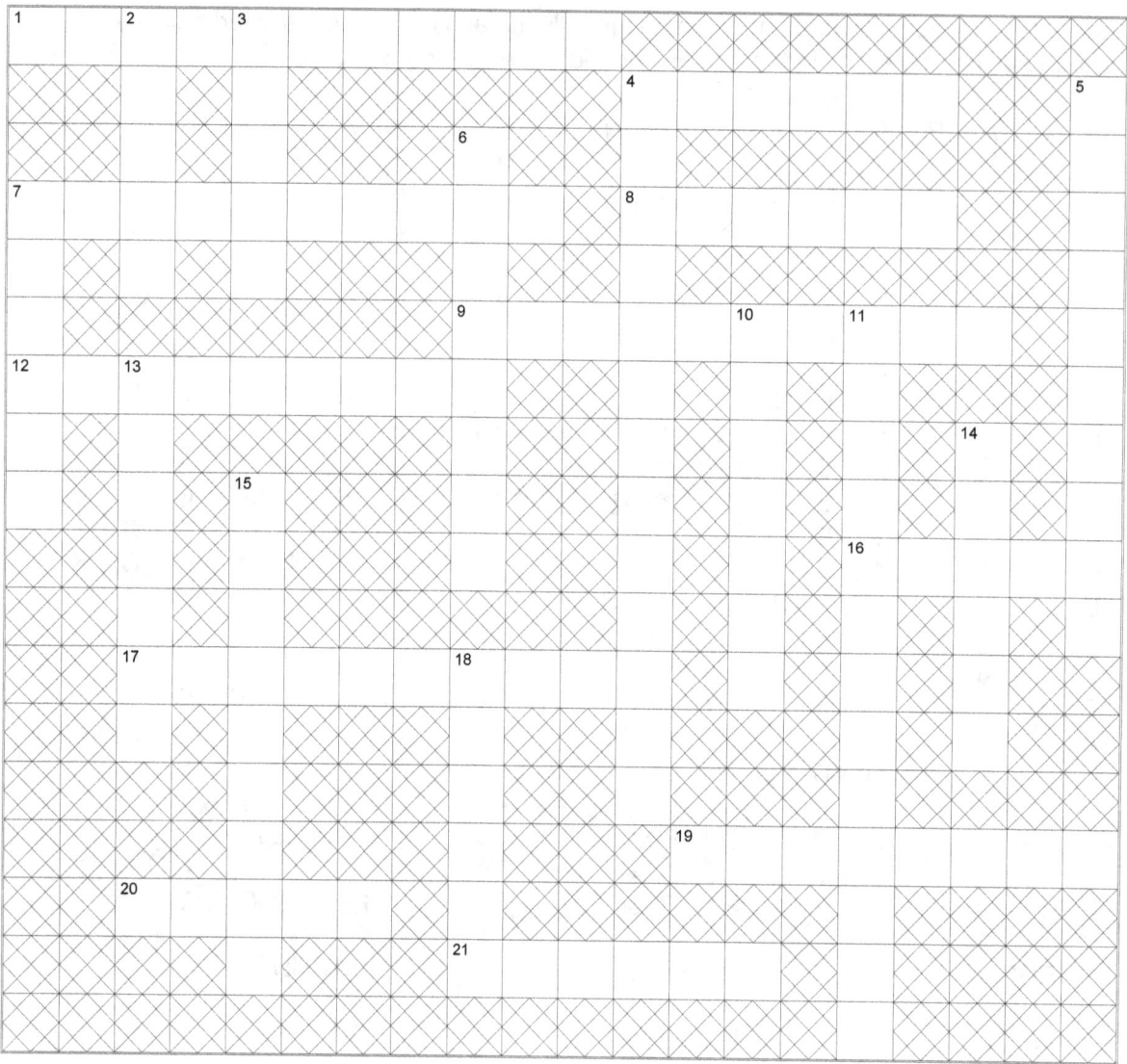

Across
1. Strong feelings of inadequacy
4. Expensive and showy
7. Mutual; equivalent; interchangeable
8. Rotten
9. Privately; personally; very closely
12. Rambles; departs temporarily from the main topic
16. Having done something so much as to be bored by it
17. Showing a lack of concern; casually indifferent
19. Meaning opposite of what is expressed
20. A person regarded as mean or contemptible
21. Lowly; unpretentious

Down
2. Coat; cloak
3. Grating
4. Worldly wise; refined
5. Shunned; excluded; left out
6. Getting pleasure from inflicting pain on others
7. Haphazardly; without careful choice; by chance
10. A person who believes there is no God
11. One who likes to show off and get attention
13. Reaching blindly
14. Feelings of doubt
15. Showing or based on total agreement
18. Generous or liberal in giving or spending

Catcher In The Rye Vocabulary Crossword 1 Answer Key

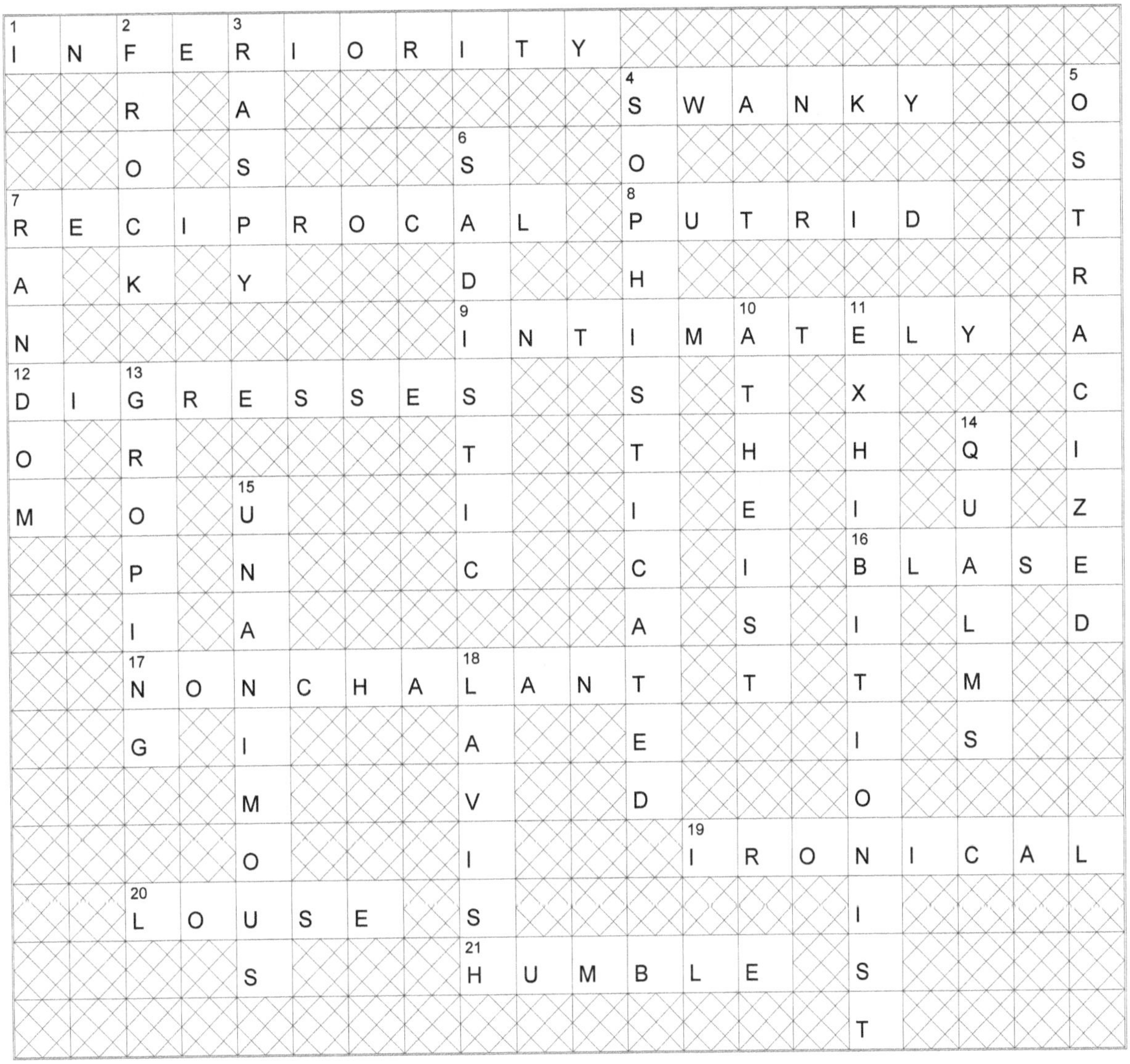

	1 I	2 N F R O C K I N D O M	3 E R A S	I	O	R	I	T	Y			
		R	A				4 S O P H I S T I C A T E D	W	A	N	K	Y	5 O S T R A C I Z E D
		O	S		6 S		O					
7 R E C I P R O C A L							8 P U T R I D					
A	K		Y		D		H					
N				9 I	N	T	I	M	A T E L Y			
12 D I G R E S S E S												

(Transcription of this crossword grid as a clean markdown table is impractical; the completed answers are listed below.)

Across
1. Strong feelings of inadequacy — INFERIORITY
4. Expensive and showy — SWANKY
7. Mutual; equivalent; interchangeable — RECIPROCAL
8. Rotten — PUTRID
9. Privately; personally; very closely — INTIMATELY
12. Rambles; departs temporarily from the main topic — DIGRESSES
16. Having done something so much as to be bored by it — BLASE
17. Showing a lack of concern; casually indifferent — NONCHALANT
19. Meaning opposite of what is expressed — IRONICAL
20. A person regarded as mean or contemptible — LOUSE
21. Lowly; unpretentious — HUMBLE

Down
2. Coat; cloak — FROCK
3. Grating — RASPY
4. Worldly wise; refined — SOPHISTICATED
5. Shunned; excluded; left out — OSTRACIZED
6. Getting pleasure from inflicting pain on others — SADISTIC
7. Haphazardly; without careful choice; by chance — RANDOM
10. A person who believes there is no God — ATHEIST
11. One who likes to show off and get attention — EXHIBITIONIST
13. Reaching blindly — GROPING
14. Feelings of doubt — QUALMS
15. Showing or based on total agreement — UNANIMOUS
18. Generous or liberal in giving or spending — LAVISH

95
Copyrighted

Catcher In The Rye Vocabulary Crossword 2

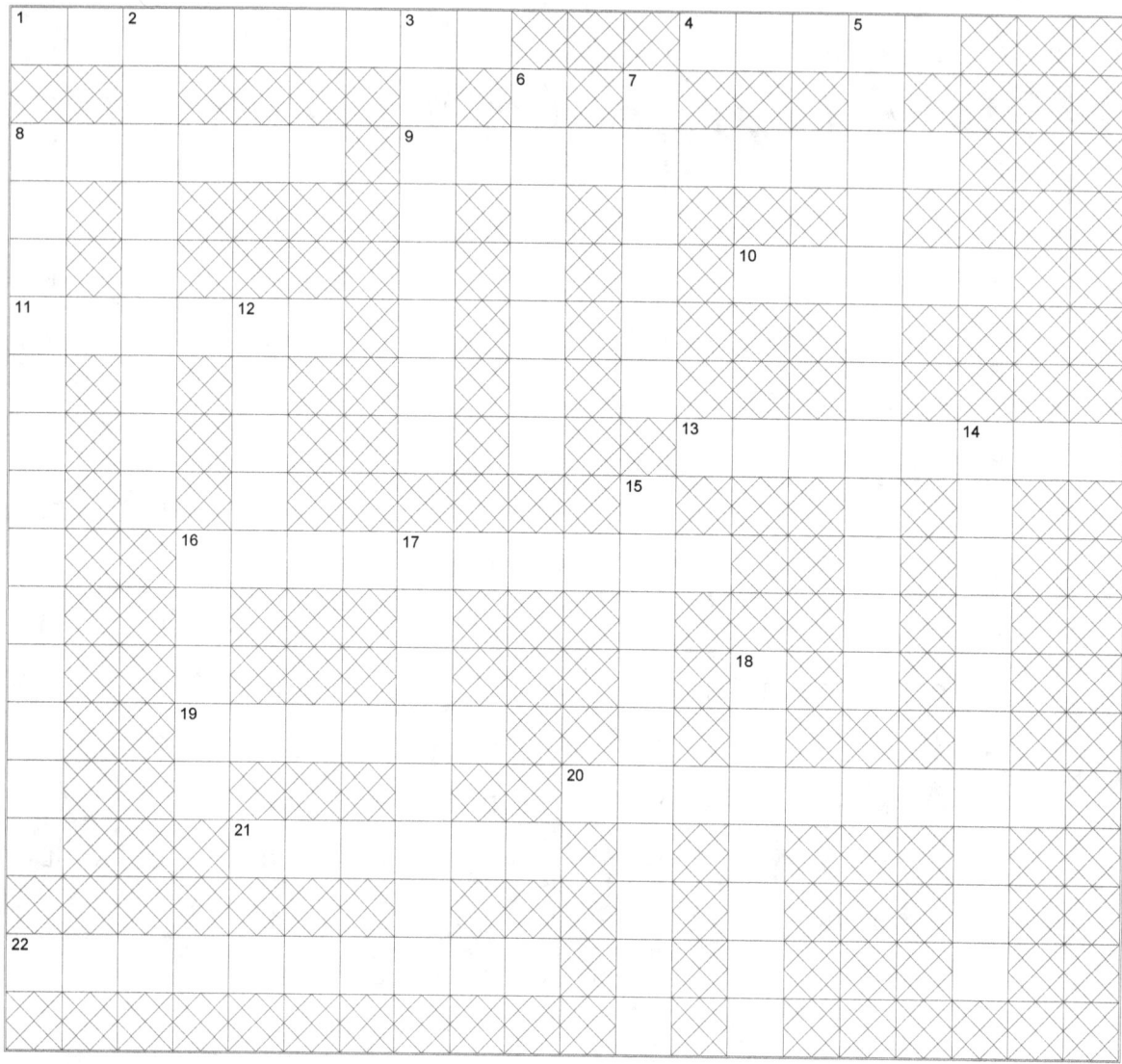

Across
1. Smug; conventional; materialistic
4. Having done something so much as to be bored by it
8. Expensive and showy
9. Shunned; excluded; left out
10. Coat; cloak
11. Lowly; unpretentious
13. Ability to contain, absorb, receive and hold
16. Mutual; equivalent; interchangeable
19. Rotten
20. In disguise
21. Generous or liberal in giving or spending
22. Often

Down
2. Showing or based on total agreement
3. Meaning opposite of what is expressed
5. A person skilled in taking shorthand
6. A person who believes there is no God
7. Haphazardly; without careful choice; by chance
8. Worldly wise; refined
12. A person regarded as mean or contemptible
14. Privately; personally; very closely
15. Held the attention of; captivated
16. Grating
17. One who opposed the use of force under any circumstances
18. Reaching blindly

Catcher In The Rye Vocabulary Crossword 2 Answer Key

Across
1. Smug; conventional; materialistic
4. Having done something so much as to be bored by it
8. Expensive and showy
9. Shunned; excluded; left out
10. Coat; cloak
11. Lowly; unpretentious
13. Ability to contain, absorb, receive and hold
16. Mutual; equivalent; interchangeable
19. Rotten
20. In disguise
21. Generous or liberal in giving or spending
22. Often

Down
2. Showing or based on total agreement
3. Meaning opposite of what is expressed
5. A person skilled in taking shorthand
6. A person who believes there is no God
7. Haphazardly; without careful choice; by chance
8. Worldly wise; refined
12. A person regarded as mean or contemptible
14. Privately; personally; very closely
15. Held the attention of; captivated
16. Grating
17. One who opposed the use of force under any circumstances
18. Reaching blindly

Catcher In The Rye Vocabulary Crossword 3

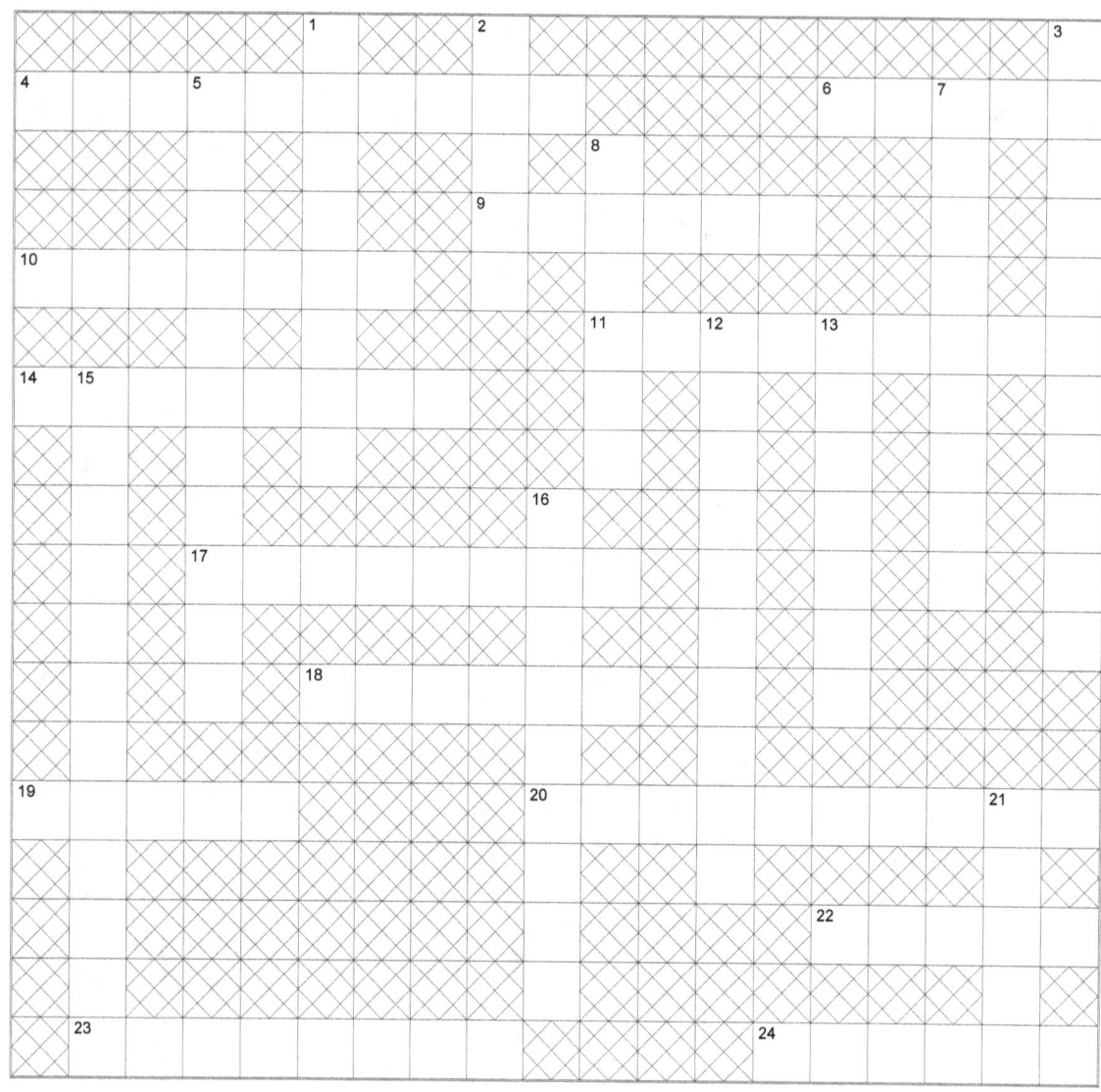

Across
4. Privately; personally; very closely
6. A person regarded as mean or contemptible
9. Expensive and showy
10. A person who believes there is no God
11. In disguise
14. One who opposed the use of force under any circumstances
17. Meaning opposite of what is expressed
18. Rotten
19. Coat; cloak
20. Shunned; excluded; left out
22. Grating
23. Ability to contain, absorb, receive and hold
24. Lowly; unpretentious

Down
1. Getting pleasure from inflicting pain on others
2. Having done something so much as to be bored by it
3. Characteristic of teaching or teachers
5. Strong feelings of inadequacy
7. Showing or based on total agreement
8. Generous or liberal in giving or spending
12. Required; must be done
13. Reaching blindly
15. Of an upper class; distinguished
16. Bad smelling breath
21. Drive out by force

Catcher In The Rye Vocabulary Crossword 3 Answer Key

Across
4. Privately; personally; very closely
6. A person regarded as mean or contemptible
9. Expensive and showy
10. A person who believes there is no God
11. In disguise
14. One who opposed the use of force under any circumstances
17. Meaning opposite of what is expressed
18. Rotten
19. Coat; cloak
20. Shunned; excluded; left out
22. Grating
23. Ability to contain, absorb, receive and hold
24. Lowly; unpretentious

Down
1. Getting pleasure from inflicting pain on others
2. Having done something so much as to be bored by it
3. Characteristic of teaching or teachers
5. Strong feelings of inadequacy
7. Showing or based on total agreement
8. Generous or liberal in giving or spending
12. Required; must be done
13. Reaching blindly
15. Of an upper class; distinguished
16. Bad smelling breath
21. Drive out by force

Catcher In The Rye Vocabulary Crossword 4

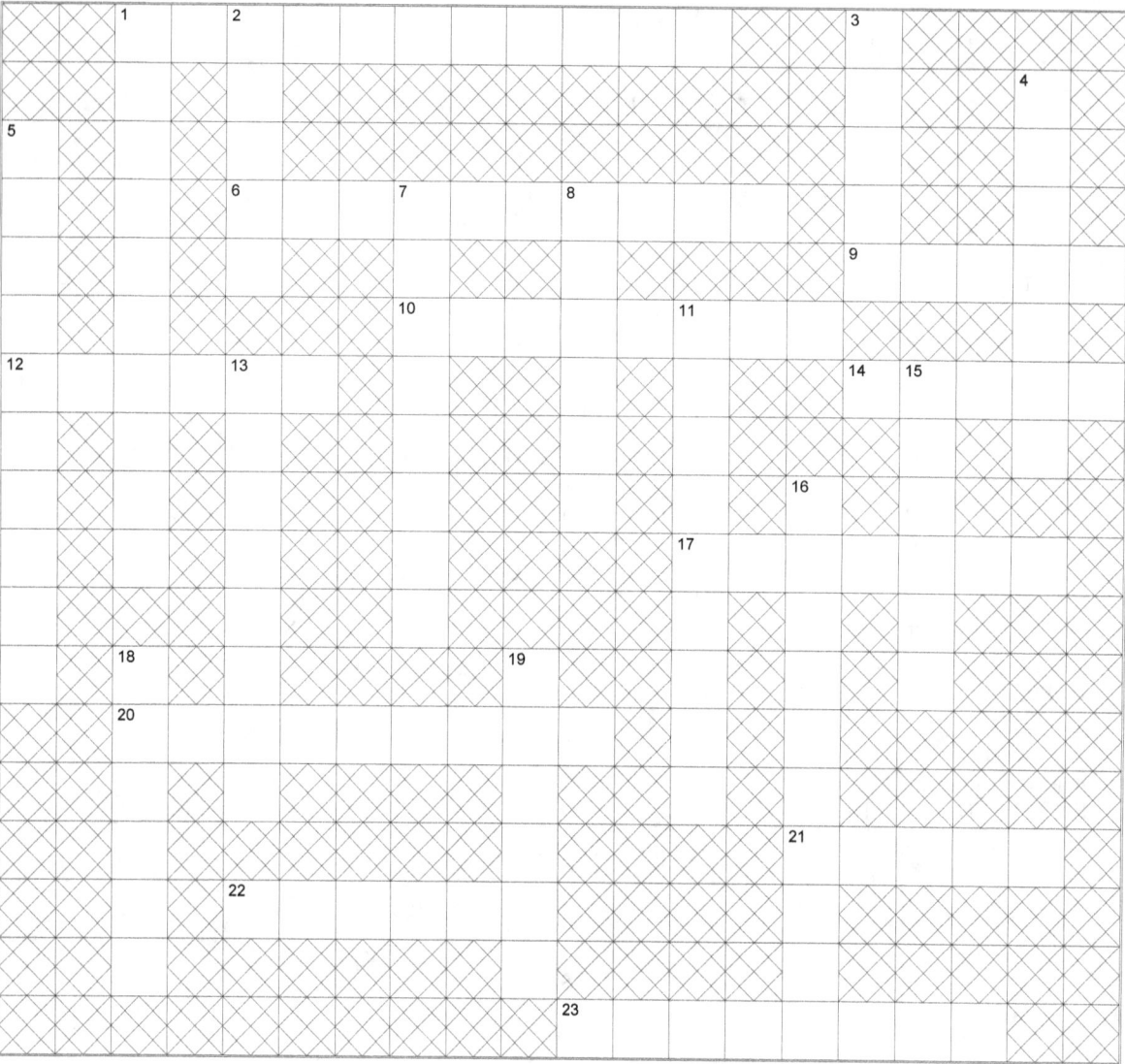

Across
1. Strong feelings of inadequacy
6. Required; must be done
9. Drive out by force
10. Ability to contain, absorb, receive and hold
12. Rotten
14. Having done something so much as to be bored by it
17. Reaching blindly
20. Showing or based on total agreement
21. Grating
22. Haphazardly; without careful choice; by chance
23. Getting pleasure from inflicting pain on others

Down
1. Privately; personally; very closely
2. Coat; cloak
3. A person regarded as mean or contemptible
4. A person who believes there is no God
5. Mutual; equivalent; interchangeable
7. One who opposed the use of force under any circumstances
8. Expensive and showy
11. In disguise
13. Meaning opposite of what is expressed
15. Generous or liberal in giving or spending
16. Noisy; unruly
18. Lowly; unpretentious
19. Feelings of doubt

Catcher In The Rye Vocabulary Crossword 4 Answer Key

Across
1. Strong feelings of inadequacy
6. Required; must be done
9. Drive out by force
10. Ability to contain, absorb, receive and hold
12. Rotten
14. Having done something so much as to be bored by it
17. Reaching blindly
20. Showing or based on total agreement
21. Grating
22. Haphazardly; without careful choice; by chance
23. Getting pleasure from inflicting pain on others

Down
1. Privately; personally; very closely
2. Coat; cloak
3. A person regarded as mean or contemptible
4. A person who believes there is no God
5. Mutual; equivalent; interchangeable
7. One who opposed the use of force under any circumstances
8. Expensive and showy
11. In disguise
13. Meaning opposite of what is expressed
15. Generous or liberal in giving or spending
16. Noisy; unruly
18. Lowly; unpretentious
19. Feelings of doubt

Catcher In The Rye Vocabulary Juggle Letters 1

1. SSIOIHTAL = 1. _____
Bad smelling breath

2. ATISFCIP = 2. _____
One who opposed the use of force under any circumstances

3. ANRMDO = 3. _____
Haphazardly; without careful choice; by chance

4. LUMQAS = 4. _____
Feelings of doubt

5. TMEANTYILI = 5. _____
Privately; personally; very closely

6. UUUOPLRSCNUS = 6. _____
Having no moral code; unprincipled

7. GNRPOGI = 7. _____
Reaching blindly

8. ROYCSMOULP = 8. _____
Required; must be done

9. OELUS = 9. _____
A person regarded as mean or contemptible

10. IOUSUANNM = 10. _____
Showing or based on total agreement

11. DFICTANSAE = 11. _____
Held the attention of; captivated

12. NRLAIOIC = 12. _____
Meaning opposite of what is expressed

13. ELPXE = 13. _____
Drive out by force

14. ORCKF = 14. _____
Coat; cloak

15. NTHAPERGSREO = 15. _____
A person skilled in taking shorthand

Catcher In The Rye Vocabulary Juggle Letters 1 Answer Key

1. SSIOIHTAL = 1. HALITOSIS
   Bad smelling breath

2. ATISFCIP = 2. PACIFIST
   One who opposed the use of force under any circumstances

3. ANRMDO = 3. RANDOM
   Haphazardly; without careful choice; by chance

4. LUMQAS = 4. QUALMS
   Feelings of doubt

5. TMEANTYILI = 5. INTIMATELY
   Privately; personally; very closely

6. UUUOPLRSCNUS = 6. UNSCRUPULOUS
   Having no moral code; unprincipled

7. GNRPOGI = 7. GROPING
   Reaching blindly

8. ROYCSMOULP = 8. COMPULSORY
   Required; must be done

9. OELUS = 9. LOUSE
   A person regarded as mean or contemptible

10. IOUSUANNM = 10. UNANIMOUS
    Showing or based on total agreement

11. DFICTANSAE = 11. FASCINATED
    Held the attention of; captivated

12. NRLAIOIC = 12. IRONICAL
    Meaning opposite of what is expressed

13. ELPXE = 13. EXPEL
    Drive out by force

14. ORCKF = 14. FROCK
    Coat; cloak

15. NTHAPERGSREO = 15. STENOGRAPHER
    A person skilled in taking shorthand

Catcher In The Rye Vocabulary Juggle Letters 2

1. CTCARIROTSIA = 1. _____
   Of an upper class; distinguished

2. AZTIDROSEC = 2. _____
   Shunned; excluded; left out

3. OASUNUMIN = 3. _____
   Showing or based on total agreement

4. YFUTNEQRLE = 4. _____
   Often

5. ALONNATNCH = 5. _____
   Showing a lack of concern; casually indifferent

6. DPGAAOLEGCI = 6. _____
   Characteristic of teaching or teachers

7. EACILPROCR = 7. _____
   Mutual; equivalent; interchangeable

8. ILSAHV = 8. _____
   Generous or liberal in giving or spending

9. YRITIFINERO = 9. _____
   Strong feelings of inadequacy

10. AMUQLS = 10. _____
    Feelings of doubt

11. CDTAEISFAN = 11. _____
    Held the attention of; captivated

12. ULEBMH = 12. _____
    Lowly; unpretentious

13. OCFRK = 13. _____
    Coat; cloak

14. ULEOS = 14. _____
    A person regarded as mean or contemptible

15. AINLYETMTI = 15. _____
    Privately; personally; very closely

Catcher In The Rye Vocabulary Juggle Letters 2 Answer Key

1. CTCARIROTSIA = 1. ARISTOCRATIC
   Of an upper class; distinguished

2. AZTIDROSEC = 2. OSTRACIZED
   Shunned; excluded; left out

3. OASUNUMIN = 3. UNANIMOUS
   Showing or based on total agreement

4. YFUTNEQRLE = 4. FREQUENTLY
   Often

5. ALONNATNCH = 5. NONCHALANT
   Showing a lack of concern; casually indifferent

6. DPGAAOLEGCI = 6. PEDAGOGICAL
   Characteristic of teaching or teachers

7. EACILPROCR = 7. RECIPROCAL
   Mutual; equivalent; interchangeable

8. ILSAHV = 8. LAVISH
   Generous or liberal in giving or spending

9. YRITIFINERO = 9. INFERIORITY
   Strong feelings of inadequacy

10. AMUQLS =10. QUALMS
    Feelings of doubt

11. CDTAEISFAN =11. FASCINATED
    Held the attention of; captivated

12. ULEBMH =12. HUMBLE
    Lowly; unpretentious

13. OCFRK =13. FROCK
    Coat; cloak

14. ULEOS =14. LOUSE
    A person regarded as mean or contemptible

15. AINLYETMTI =15. INTIMATELY
    Privately; personally; very closely

Catcher In The Rye Vocabulary Juggle Letters 3

1. RSESIGDES = 1. _____
Rambles; departs temporarily from the main topic

2. CPRSOUULNUSU = 2. _____
Having no moral code; unprincipled

3. ISHAVL = 3. _____
Generous or liberal in giving or spending

4. TCNONGIIO = 4. _____
In disguise

5. IATOHSSLI = 5. _____
Bad smelling breath

6. TFEUQRELYN = 6. _____
Often

7. EYLAMTINTI = 7. _____
Privately; personally; very closely

8. GPNIGOR = 8. _____
Reaching blindly

9. SLEAB = 9. _____
Having done something so much as to be bored by it

10. TCPCAYAI =10. _____
Ability to contain, absorb, receive and hold

11. OCYULOPMSR =11. _____
Required; must be done

12. OCARLINI =12. _____
Meaning opposite of what is expressed

13. NSONESIUCCIOT =13. _____
Attentive to duty; diligent

14. OUSLE =14. _____
A person regarded as mean or contemptible

15. COCITRTAISAR =15. _____
Of an upper class; distinguished

Catcher In The Rye Vocabulary Juggle Letters 3 Answer Key

1. RSESIGDES = 1. DIGRESSES
Rambles; departs temporarily from the main topic

2. CPRSOUULNUSU = 2. UNSCRUPULOUS
Having no moral code; unprincipled

3. ISHAVL = 3. LAVISH
Generous or liberal in giving or spending

4. TCNONGIIO = 4. INCOGNITO
In disguise

5. IATOHSSLI = 5. HALITOSIS
Bad smelling breath

6. TFEUQRELYN = 6. FREQUENTLY
Often

7. EYLAMTINTI = 7. INTIMATELY
Privately; personally; very closely

8. GPNIGOR = 8. GROPING
Reaching blindly

9. SLEAB = 9. BLASE
Having done something so much as to be bored by it

10. TCPCAYAI = 10. CAPACITY
Ability to contain, absorb, receive and hold

11. OCYULOPMSR = 11. COMPULSORY
Required; must be done

12. OCARLINI = 12. IRONICAL
Meaning opposite of what is expressed

13. NSONESIUCCIOT = 13. CONSCIENTIOUS
Attentive to duty; diligent

14. OUSLE = 14. LOUSE
A person regarded as mean or contemptible

15. COCITRTAISAR = 15. ARISTOCRATIC
Of an upper class; distinguished

Copyrighted

Catcher In The Rye Vocabulary Juggle Letters 4

1. OAEDCPIGLAG = 1. _____
Characteristic of teaching or teachers

2. HAISTET = 2. _____
A person who believes there is no God

3. DCIFESNAAT = 3. _____
Held the attention of; captivated

4. CSUULPSURONU = 4. _____
Having no moral code; unprincipled

5. KAWYSN = 5. _____
Expensive and showy

6. GRSHENAEOTRP = 6. _____
A person skilled in taking shorthand

7. OFRYEITRNII = 7. _____
Strong feelings of inadequacy

8. RTDIUP = 8. _____
Rotten

9. EULSO = 9. _____
A person regarded as mean or contemptible

10. SESERGIDS =10. _____
Rambles; departs temporarily from the main topic

11. HCPTSOSTAEDII =11. _____
Worldly wise; refined

12. TCIOCTRARIAS =12. _____
Of an upper class; distinguished

13. XITBIETHINOSI =13. _____
One who likes to show off and get attention

14. UROIOBESG =14. _____
Smug; conventional; materialistic

15. LASIVH =15. _____
Generous or liberal in giving or spending

Catcher In The Rye Vocabulary Juggle Letters 4 Answer Key

1. OAEDCPIGLAG = 1. PEDAGOGICAL
   Characteristic of teaching or teachers

2. HAISTET = 2. ATHEIST
   A person who believes there is no God

3. DCIFESNAAT = 3. FASCINATED
   Held the attention of; captivated

4. CSUULPSURONU = 4. UNSCRUPULOUS
   Having no moral code; unprincipled

5. KAWYSN = 5. SWANKY
   Expensive and showy

6. GRSHENAEOTRP = 6. STENOGRAPHER
   A person skilled in taking shorthand

7. OFRYEITRNII = 7. INFERIORITY
   Strong feelings of inadequacy

8. RTDIUP = 8. PUTRID
   Rotten

9. EULSO = 9. LOUSE
   A person regarded as mean or contemptible

10. SESERGIDS = 10. DIGRESSES
    Rambles; departs temporarily from the main topic

11. HCPTSOSTAEDII = 11. SOPHISTICATED
    Worldly wise; refined

12. TCIOCTRARIAS = 12. ARISTOCRATIC
    Of an upper class; distinguished

13. XITBIETHINOSI = 13. EXHIBITIONIST
    One who likes to show off and get attention

14. UROIOBESG = 14. BOURGEOIS
    Smug; conventional; materialistic

15. LASIVH = 15. LAVISH
    Generous or liberal in giving or spending

ARISTOCRATIC	Of an upper class; distinguished
ATHEIST	A person who believes there is no God
BLASE	Having done something so much as to be bored by it
BOISTEROUS	Noisy; unruly
BOURGEOIS	Smug; conventional; materialistic
CAPACITY	Ability to contain, absorb, receive and hold

COMPULSORY	Required; must be done
CONSCIENTIOUS	Attentive to duty; diligent
DIGRESSES	Rambles; departs temporarily from the main topic
EXHIBITIONIST	One who likes to show off and get attention
EXPEL	Drive out by force
FASCINATED	Held the attention of; captivated

FREQUENTLY	Often
FROCK	Coat; cloak
GROPING	Reaching blindly
HALITOSIS	Bad smelling breath
HEMORRHAGES	Bursting of blood vessels
HUMBLE	Lowly; unpretentious

INCOGNITO	In disguise
INFERIORITY	Strong feelings of inadequacy
INTIMATELY	Privately; personally; very closely
IRONICAL	Meaning opposite of what is expressed
LAVISH	Generous or liberal in giving or spending
LOUSE	A person regarded as mean or contemptible

NONCHALANT	Showing a lack of concern; casually indifferent
OSTRACIZED	Shunned; excluded; left out
PACIFIST	One who opposed the use of force under any circumstances
PEDAGOGICAL	Characteristic of teaching or teachers
PUTRID	Rotten
QUALMS	Feelings of doubt

RANDOM	Haphazardly; without careful choice; by chance
RASPY	Grating
RECIPROCAL	Mutual; equivalent; interchangeable
SADISTIC	Getting pleasure from inflicting pain on others
SOPHISTICATED	Worldly wise; refined
STENOGRAPHER	A person skilled in taking shorthand

SWANKY	Expensive and showy
UNANIMOUS	Showing or based on total agreement
UNSCRUPULOUS	Having no moral code; unprincipled

Catcher In The Rye Vocabulary

BLASE	GROPING	ARISTOCRATIC	COMPULSORY	PACIFIST
HEMORRHAGES	INTIMATELY	STENOGRAPHER	FROCK	UNSCRUPULOUS
IRONICAL	ATHEIST	FREE SPACE	SADISTIC	LOUSE
FREQUENTLY	BOISTEROUS	DIGRESSES	BOURGEOIS	HUMBLE
OSTRACIZED	LAVISH	HALITOSIS	EXPEL	CONSCIENTIOUS

Catcher In The Rye Vocabulary

SWANKY	PUTRID	QUALMS	EXHIBITIONIST	INCOGNITO
PEDAGOGICAL	RASPY	CAPACITY	SOPHISTICATED	RANDOM
RECIPROCAL	UNANIMOUS	FREE SPACE	NONCHALANT	CONSCIENTIOUS
EXPEL	HALITOSIS	LAVISH	OSTRACIZED	HUMBLE
BOURGEOIS	DIGRESSES	BOISTEROUS	FREQUENTLY	LOUSE

Catcher In The Rye Vocabulary

BOISTEROUS	LOUSE	HUMBLE	DIGRESSES	COMPULSORY
HEMORRHAGES	QUALMS	IRONICAL	FASCINATED	EXHIBITIONIST
SADISTIC	LAVISH	FREE SPACE	SWANKY	UNANIMOUS
BOURGEOIS	HALITOSIS	OSTRACIZED	FREQUENTLY	INFERIORITY
INTIMATELY	PACIFIST	STENOGRAPHER	PEDAGOGICAL	FROCK

Catcher In The Rye Vocabulary

CAPACITY	EXPEL	BLASE	GROPING	RASPY
UNSCRUPULOUS	SOPHISTICATED	PUTRID	CONSCIENTIOUS	INCOGNITO
ATHEIST	NONCHALANT	FREE SPACE	ARISTOCRATIC	FROCK
PEDAGOGICAL	STENOGRAPHER	PACIFIST	INTIMATELY	INFERIORITY
FREQUENTLY	OSTRACIZED	HALITOSIS	BOURGEOIS	UNANIMOUS

Catcher In The Rye Vocabulary

DIGRESSES	IRONICAL	INFERIORITY	RECIPROCAL	EXHIBITIONIST
BOISTEROUS	ARISTOCRATIC	HEMORRHAGES	FREQUENTLY	RASPY
PUTRID	HUMBLE	FREE SPACE	PEDAGOGICAL	CAPACITY
NONCHALANT	LAVISH	BLASE	QUALMS	INCOGNITO
COMPULSORY	UNANIMOUS	UNSCRUPULOUS	GROPING	SWANKY

Catcher In The Rye Vocabulary

RANDOM	ATHEIST	EXPEL	CONSCIENTIOUS	FROCK
PACIFIST	SADISTIC	BOURGEOIS	STENOGRAPHER	SOPHISTICATED
LOUSE	HALITOSIS	FREE SPACE	OSTRACIZED	SWANKY
GROPING	UNSCRUPULOUS	UNANIMOUS	COMPULSORY	INCOGNITO
QUALMS	BLASE	LAVISH	NONCHALANT	CAPACITY

Catcher In The Rye Vocabulary

GROPING	COMPULSORY	HALITOSIS	RECIPROCAL	QUALMS
OSTRACIZED	IRONICAL	PUTRID	STENOGRAPHER	DIGRESSES
FASCINATED	PEDAGOGICAL	FREE SPACE	UNANIMOUS	RANDOM
BOISTEROUS	INTIMATELY	ATHEIST	LAVISH	RASPY
INFERIORITY	SADISTIC	CAPACITY	SOPHISTICATED	FROCK

Catcher In The Rye Vocabulary

EXHIBITIONIST	NONCHALANT	CONSCIENTIOUS	UNSCRUPULOUS	FREQUENTLY
LOUSE	EXPEL	PACIFIST	BOURGEOIS	HUMBLE
SWANKY	HEMORRHAGES	FREE SPACE	ARISTOCRATIC	FROCK
SOPHISTICATED	CAPACITY	SADISTIC	INFERIORITY	RASPY
LAVISH	ATHEIST	INTIMATELY	BOISTEROUS	RANDOM

Catcher In The Rye Vocabulary

EXHIBITIONIST	INCOGNITO	RANDOM	CAPACITY	INFERIORITY
BOISTEROUS	NONCHALANT	OSTRACIZED	SWANKY	HUMBLE
FREQUENTLY	PEDAGOGICAL	FREE SPACE	FASCINATED	EXPEL
INTIMATELY	STENOGRAPHER	DIGRESSES	IRONICAL	PACIFIST
BOURGEOIS	SADISTIC	FROCK	COMPULSORY	UNSCRUPULOUS

Catcher In The Rye Vocabulary

QUALMS	ARISTOCRATIC	RASPY	PUTRID	BLASE
LOUSE	ATHEIST	UNANIMOUS	SOPHISTICATED	RECIPROCAL
GROPING	HALITOSIS	FREE SPACE	HEMORRHAGES	UNSCRUPULOUS
COMPULSORY	FROCK	SADISTIC	BOURGEOIS	PACIFIST
IRONICAL	DIGRESSES	STENOGRAPHER	INTIMATELY	EXPEL

Catcher In The Rye Vocabulary

PEDAGOGICAL	ATHEIST	RANDOM	ARISTOCRATIC	INTIMATELY
NONCHALANT	UNANIMOUS	LOUSE	EXHIBITIONIST	STENOGRAPHER
COMPULSORY	DIGRESSES	FREE SPACE	IRONICAL	RECIPROCAL
GROPING	HALITOSIS	BLASE	OSTRACIZED	EXPEL
HEMORRHAGES	HUMBLE	QUALMS	RASPY	UNSCRUPULOUS

Catcher In The Rye Vocabulary

BOISTEROUS	INFERIORITY	FROCK	INCOGNITO	SWANKY
CONSCIENTIOUS	FASCINATED	SADISTIC	PUTRID	BOURGEOIS
SOPHISTICATED	FREQUENTLY	FREE SPACE	PACIFIST	UNSCRUPULOUS
RASPY	QUALMS	HUMBLE	HEMORRHAGES	EXPEL
OSTRACIZED	BLASE	HALITOSIS	GROPING	RECIPROCAL

Catcher In The Rye Vocabulary

CAPACITY	SADISTIC	DIGRESSES	UNANIMOUS	BLASE
BOURGEOIS	HUMBLE	PEDAGOGICAL	SWANKY	CONSCIENTIOUS
SOPHISTICATED	NONCHALANT	FREE SPACE	ATHEIST	INTIMATELY
INFERIORITY	UNSCRUPULOUS	OSTRACIZED	EXPEL	FREQUENTLY
ARISTOCRATIC	QUALMS	EXHIBITIONIST	IRONICAL	LOUSE

Catcher In The Rye Vocabulary

INCOGNITO	FASCINATED	GROPING	RECIPROCAL	RASPY
BOISTEROUS	HALITOSIS	PUTRID	PACIFIST	RANDOM
LAVISH	STENOGRAPHER	FREE SPACE	COMPULSORY	LOUSE
IRONICAL	EXHIBITIONIST	QUALMS	ARISTOCRATIC	FREQUENTLY
EXPEL	OSTRACIZED	UNSCRUPULOUS	INFERIORITY	INTIMATELY

Catcher In The Rye Vocabulary

RANDOM	INFERIORITY	PACIFIST	BLASE	SWANKY
COMPULSORY	FASCINATED	LOUSE	CONSCIENTIOUS	STENOGRAPHER
HUMBLE	CAPACITY	FREE SPACE	SOPHISTICATED	EXPEL
OSTRACIZED	FREQUENTLY	ARISTOCRATIC	SADISTIC	DIGRESSES
UNSCRUPULOUS	GROPING	QUALMS	RASPY	UNANIMOUS

Catcher In The Rye Vocabulary

FROCK	HALITOSIS	PUTRID	BOURGEOIS	PEDAGOGICAL
NONCHALANT	HEMORRHAGES	EXHIBITIONIST	INCOGNITO	RECIPROCAL
ATHEIST	INTIMATELY	FREE SPACE	IRONICAL	UNANIMOUS
RASPY	QUALMS	GROPING	UNSCRUPULOUS	DIGRESSES
SADISTIC	ARISTOCRATIC	FREQUENTLY	OSTRACIZED	EXPEL

Catcher In The Rye Vocabulary

PACIFIST	RANDOM	PUTRID	CAPACITY	FROCK
FASCINATED	UNANIMOUS	INCOGNITO	EXPEL	LOUSE
SOPHISTICATED	BLASE	FREE SPACE	UNSCRUPULOUS	LAVISH
ATHEIST	HUMBLE	COMPULSORY	SADISTIC	RECIPROCAL
EXHIBITIONIST	NONCHALANT	DIGRESSES	HEMORRHAGES	QUALMS

Catcher In The Rye Vocabulary

ARISTOCRATIC	BOISTEROUS	BOURGEOIS	IRONICAL	CONSCIENTIOUS
STENOGRAPHER	SWANKY	PEDAGOGICAL	INTIMATELY	FREQUENTLY
INFERIORITY	OSTRACIZED	FREE SPACE	HALITOSIS	QUALMS
HEMORRHAGES	DIGRESSES	NONCHALANT	EXHIBITIONIST	RECIPROCAL
SADISTIC	COMPULSORY	HUMBLE	ATHEIST	LAVISH

Catcher In The Rye Vocabulary

PACIFIST	ATHEIST	COMPULSORY	RANDOM	IRONICAL
FREQUENTLY	HUMBLE	PUTRID	SOPHISTICATED	FASCINATED
CAPACITY	INTIMATELY	FREE SPACE	CONSCIENTIOUS	BOURGEOIS
SWANKY	EXHIBITIONIST	BOISTEROUS	GROPING	ARISTOCRATIC
FROCK	INCOGNITO	SADISTIC	HEMORRHAGES	QUALMS

Catcher In The Rye Vocabulary

DIGRESSES	BLASE	HALITOSIS	STENOGRAPHER	OSTRACIZED
LAVISH	LOUSE	UNSCRUPULOUS	RECIPROCAL	RASPY
NONCHALANT	PEDAGOGICAL	FREE SPACE	UNANIMOUS	QUALMS
HEMORRHAGES	SADISTIC	INCOGNITO	FROCK	ARISTOCRATIC
GROPING	BOISTEROUS	EXHIBITIONIST	SWANKY	BOURGEOIS

Catcher In The Rye Vocabulary

RANDOM	NONCHALANT	RASPY	DIGRESSES	FROCK
COMPULSORY	LAVISH	QUALMS	EXPEL	BOISTEROUS
SWANKY	INCOGNITO	FREE SPACE	IRONICAL	FASCINATED
INFERIORITY	PACIFIST	INTIMATELY	PUTRID	FREQUENTLY
STENOGRAPHER	SOPHISTICATED	CAPACITY	GROPING	BLASE

Catcher In The Rye Vocabulary

HALITOSIS	PEDAGOGICAL	CONSCIENTIOUS	UNSCRUPULOUS	ATHEIST
EXHIBITIONIST	ARISTOCRATIC	BOURGEOIS	RECIPROCAL	LOUSE
SADISTIC	HEMORRHAGES	FREE SPACE	OSTRACIZED	BLASE
GROPING	CAPACITY	SOPHISTICATED	STENOGRAPHER	FREQUENTLY
PUTRID	INTIMATELY	PACIFIST	INFERIORITY	FASCINATED

Catcher In The Rye Vocabulary

UNANIMOUS	EXHIBITIONIST	NONCHALANT	BOURGEOIS	INFERIORITY
RASPY	DIGRESSES	RECIPROCAL	OSTRACIZED	HEMORRHAGES
SWANKY	FROCK	FREE SPACE	QUALMS	HALITOSIS
PACIFIST	COMPULSORY	INTIMATELY	BLASE	INCOGNITO
PEDAGOGICAL	ARISTOCRATIC	SOPHISTICATED	HUMBLE	SADISTIC

Catcher In The Rye Vocabulary

BOISTEROUS	UNSCRUPULOUS	CONSCIENTIOUS	CAPACITY	LOUSE
IRONICAL	LAVISH	ATHEIST	EXPEL	RANDOM
STENOGRAPHER	PUTRID	FREE SPACE	FREQUENTLY	SADISTIC
HUMBLE	SOPHISTICATED	ARISTOCRATIC	PEDAGOGICAL	INCOGNITO
BLASE	INTIMATELY	COMPULSORY	PACIFIST	HALITOSIS

Catcher In The Rye Vocabulary

FROCK	ARISTOCRATIC	INCOGNITO	INFERIORITY	CAPACITY
NONCHALANT	EXPEL	HALITOSIS	BOISTEROUS	FASCINATED
PEDAGOGICAL	EXHIBITIONIST	FREE SPACE	PUTRID	LAVISH
RECIPROCAL	GROPING	OSTRACIZED	STENOGRAPHER	COMPULSORY
CONSCIENTIOUS	RASPY	SOPHISTICATED	IRONICAL	ATHEIST

Catcher In The Rye Vocabulary

SADISTIC	DIGRESSES	UNSCRUPULOUS	PACIFIST	QUALMS
HEMORRHAGES	HUMBLE	UNANIMOUS	BLASE	FREQUENTLY
SWANKY	LOUSE	FREE SPACE	BOURGEOIS	ATHEIST
IRONICAL	SOPHISTICATED	RASPY	CONSCIENTIOUS	COMPULSORY
STENOGRAPHER	OSTRACIZED	GROPING	RECIPROCAL	LAVISH

Catcher In The Rye Vocabulary

OSTRACIZED	RASPY	PUTRID	ARISTOCRATIC	HUMBLE
IRONICAL	BLASE	LOUSE	ATHEIST	RECIPROCAL
FASCINATED	LAVISH	FREE SPACE	SOPHISTICATED	INCOGNITO
PACIFIST	STENOGRAPHER	CONSCIENTIOUS	EXPEL	EXHIBITIONIST
HEMORRHAGES	FREQUENTLY	INFERIORITY	DIGRESSES	SADISTIC

Catcher In The Rye Vocabulary

NONCHALANT	CAPACITY	UNANIMOUS	INTIMATELY	UNSCRUPULOUS
GROPING	BOURGEOIS	FROCK	PEDAGOGICAL	BOISTEROUS
HALITOSIS	QUALMS	FREE SPACE	COMPULSORY	SADISTIC
DIGRESSES	INFERIORITY	FREQUENTLY	HEMORRHAGES	EXHIBITIONIST
EXPEL	CONSCIENTIOUS	STENOGRAPHER	PACIFIST	INCOGNITO

Catcher In The Rye Vocabulary

SWANKY	LAVISH	COMPULSORY	DIGRESSES	BOURGEOIS
RANDOM	IRONICAL	BOISTEROUS	BLASE	CONSCIENTIOUS
PUTRID	QUALMS	FREE SPACE	HALITOSIS	EXPEL
LOUSE	OSTRACIZED	RASPY	EXHIBITIONIST	SADISTIC
UNSCRUPULOUS	GROPING	ARISTOCRATIC	FROCK	PEDAGOGICAL

Catcher In The Rye Vocabulary

FASCINATED	RECIPROCAL	UNANIMOUS	ATHEIST	NONCHALANT
INFERIORITY	INCOGNITO	HEMORRHAGES	PACIFIST	INTIMATELY
HUMBLE	FREQUENTLY	FREE SPACE	STENOGRAPHER	PEDAGOGICAL
FROCK	ARISTOCRATIC	GROPING	UNSCRUPULOUS	SADISTIC
EXHIBITIONIST	RASPY	OSTRACIZED	LOUSE	EXPEL

Catcher In The Rye Vocabulary

FREQUENTLY	FASCINATED	HEMORRHAGES	LAVISH	UNANIMOUS
EXHIBITIONIST	FROCK	RASPY	PUTRID	BLASE
CONSCIENTIOUS	BOURGEOIS	FREE SPACE	STENOGRAPHER	RANDOM
EXPEL	RECIPROCAL	CAPACITY	NONCHALANT	ARISTOCRATIC
HALITOSIS	SWANKY	OSTRACIZED	BOISTEROUS	PACIFIST

Catcher In The Rye Vocabulary

UNSCRUPULOUS	INCOGNITO	COMPULSORY	INTIMATELY	INFERIORITY
SADISTIC	PEDAGOGICAL	HUMBLE	GROPING	QUALMS
ATHEIST	LOUSE	FREE SPACE	SOPHISTICATED	PACIFIST
BOISTEROUS	OSTRACIZED	SWANKY	HALITOSIS	ARISTOCRATIC
NONCHALANT	CAPACITY	RECIPROCAL	EXPEL	RANDOM